Stephen Rush, Editor

With an Introduction by Roland B. Smith

The *Leadership in Action* Series

ON SELECTING, DEVELOPING, AND MANAGING TALENT

CENTER FOR CREATIVE LEADERSHIP
Greensboro, North Carolina

CCL Stock Number 197

Published by CCL Press
Sylvester Taylor, Director of Assessments, Tools, and Publications
Peter Scisco, Manager, Publication Development
Stephen Rush, Editor
Karen Lewis, Editor

Design and layout by Joanne Ferguson

Library of Congress Cataloging-in-Publication Data

On selecting, developing, and managing talent / Stephen Rush, editor ; with an introduction by Roland B. Smith.
p. cm. — (The leadership in action series)
Includes bibliographical references and index.
ISBN 978-1-60491-143-5 (print on demand : alk. paper) — ISBN 978-1-60491-144-2 (e-book) 1. Leadership. 2. Leadership—Psychological aspects. I. Rush, Stephen, 1954-

HD57.7.O4957 2012
658.3—dc23

2012023662

Center for Creative Leadership

www.ccl.org

The Center for Creative Leadership is an international, nonprofit educational institution founded in 1970 to advance the understanding, practice, and development of leadership for the benefit of society worldwide. As a part of this mission, it publishes books and reports that aim to contribute to a general process of inquiry and understanding in which ideas related to leadership are raised, exchanged, and evaluated. The ideas presented in its publications are those of the author or authors.

The Center thanks you for supporting its work through the purchase of this volume. If you have comments, suggestions, or questions about any CCL Press publications, please contact the Director of Publications at the address given below.

Center for Creative Leadership
Post Office Box 26300
Greensboro, North Carolina 27438-6300
Telephone 336 288 7210
www.ccl.org

CONTENTS

INTRODUCTION

For most organizations, selecting, developing, and managing talent are critical factors for success now and in the future. CCL's research and interviews with senior executives have consistently identified the cultivation of next-generation leaders as one of the crucial challenges facing organizations. Similarly, The Conference Board has regularly pinpointed addressing human capital issues as a priority for organizations. Organizations need to be more strategic with regard to growing talent internally, improving leadership development programs, and providing training and development more broadly to employees. But human capital and talent infrastructure are only part of the equation.

If you are in a leadership position in an organization, chances are that you are thinking about, acting on, and struggling with some aspect of talent management. Talent management has become one of the most demanding organizational tasks of our time. It includes efforts to attract, select, develop, engage, and retain valuable employees. However, I believe that individual leaders and organizations need to focus less on talent management and more on talent sustainability, because whereas talent management is a process, talent sustainability should be the outcome. Talent sustainability is an organization's ability to continuously attract, select, manage, engage, and retain people needed for current and future organizational success.

Note that there are two important aspects of this definition. First is the word *continuously*. Organizations are seeking to make talent sustainability a core organizational capability that endures shifts in organizational strategy and changes in the external environment. Second is the emphasis on not only people's *capabilities* but also their *commitment*. Organizations want to employ people who not only have the necessary talent but also are fully engaged in the organization's work. They recognize that they need to focus on both current and future talent needs.

My experiences in working with senior executives have reinforced my belief that they need help in learning to effectively pull the talent lever and establish the right culture in order to achieve the strategic objectives of the enterprise. This fieldbook is intended to provide that help so your organization can not merely survive but thrive in the future.

This book is comprised of revised and updated versions of articles originally published in CCL's magazine, *Leadership in Action*, between 2000 and 2010. It is the third installment in CCL's The *Leadership in Action* Series; the first two are titled *On Strategic Leadership* and *On Leading in Times of Change*. Future topics will include Leading the Global Organization, Innovation and Creativity, Coaching and Mentoring, and more.

This entire fieldbook is a must-read but is also written in a way that will allow you to focus on your area of interest or need. Following are brief summaries of some of the perspectives found in this volume:

- David Berke, Michael Kossler, and Michael Wakefield share a basic framework that can be used to create a leadership development process.
- Robin Authey and Robert Burnside describe the challenges faced by organizations seeking to engage employees and go on to provide eight helpful approaches to engagement.
- Berke explores the definition of the high-potential employee and discusses what it means from both an organizational and individual perspective.
- Anjali Hazarika gives examples of the need for robust succession systems and focusing on building the capability of your people by sharing the journey of Oil India Limited (OIL) in a time of significant growth for the company.
- Robert Hogan and Robert Kaiser discuss the topic of CEO selection and revisit three reoccurring problems associated with executive selection.

- Barbara Neisendorf and Scott Saslow also chime in on the challenges of identifying the right senior executive, focusing their discussion on the importance of involving the board in CEO-selection decisions.
- Alessia D'Amato and Kelly Hannum share insights from CCL's research exploring what younger and older workers want from their leaders, discussing similarities and differences between the groups.
- David Baldwin and Stephanie Trovas explore the world of emerging leaders in organizations and discuss ways to more effectively support this group.
- Kris Downing discusses the implications of the fact that in today's workforce, four generations of workers are intermingled, including the most recent, the Millennials. She looks at ways to best engage the Millennials and create a culture that works across generations.
- Strategy, culture, and talent are three aspects of organizational transformation. Vidula Bal and Laura Quinn focus on the aspect that is often neglected—culture—providing several examples to illustrate that attention to both formal development and organizational culture are key to success.
- Robert Hogan and Robert Kaiser suggest that individual managers need not only a general awareness and understanding of human nature but also a more formalized knowledge of personality in the workplace. They also reinforce that one of the main keys to effective leadership and understanding others is self-awareness.
- Maxine Dalton posits that although individuals clearly have personal responsibility for their own development, others have significant roles to play in enhancing that development. Specifically, managers play a critical role in

developing talented people and can have a considerable impact on the enterprise by strengthening the talent pool.

- It is often assumed that leaders got where they are by virtue of good character; however, this is sometimes not the case. Gene Klann writes that although the issue of developing character may be controversial, there are ways for organizations to embrace approaches that identify, strengthen, and reinforce character.
- The competition to retain talented people, especially leaders, will intensify over the next decade. Karen Bryson and Karissa McKenna point out that knowing what the various generations want and need in the workplace can provide an edge in that battle.
- What approaches do organizations follow when replacing their most senior executives? Berke explores a couple of models and shares important knowledge about who should be engaged in the process to increase the potential for success.
- Finally, Michael Jenkins looks at talent management in the rising economies of the Asia-Pacific region. The implications are important for organizations not only in Asia-Pacific but also around the world.

As you can see, this fieldbook is not only thought-provoking but also a tool to help your organization navigate the challenges associated with talent. I am sure you will find some answers and will be able to share some successes with us in the future.

Roland B. Smith
Senior Faculty and Lead Researcher
Global Talent and Senior Executive Research Initiatives
Center for Creative Leadership

Building Talent: Developing Effective Leaders Is as Crucial as Ever

David Berke, Michael E. Kossler, and Michael Wakefield

Even in the midst of economic upheaval, some organizations recognize that making sure they have the right leadership talent in place will help them not only survive but thrive when the economy eventually rebounds. Developing leadership talent requires a systematic approach that begins with the organization's strategic goals and takes into account developmental needs at both the organizational and individual levels.

For years now the buzz in the business world has been that talent is the most important corporate resource. The reason? Because talent is and will continue to be a scarce resource. Baby boomers are on the brink of retirement, and there are not enough Generation Xers to replace them. But recent events seem to have diminished the concern about talent, as organizations around the world laid off thousands of people in response to the global economic crisis.

Predictably, many organizations now are choosing to delay or cancel development efforts needed to groom their future leaders. Other organizations, however, recognize that the ability to develop effective leaders remains critical to achieving competitive advantage. One of the key findings of McKinsey & Company's seminal 1997 research report "The War for Talent" was that on average, companies that were more successful in attracting, developing, and retaining talented managers had a 22 percent higher return to shareholders. Fifteen years later the McKinsey research remains relevant and valid.

Consider Internet networking and communications equipment giant Cisco Systems. In the December 2008 issue of *Fast Company* magazine, Cisco Chairman and CEO John Chambers discussed the importance of continuing to develop talent even during times of economic downturn. Cisco was greatly affected by the dot-com bust that started in 2000. But today, in the midst of an even wider economic downturn, Cisco appears to be flourishing. Chambers attributes Cisco's current stability to lessons learned, a radical change in the company's organizational culture (initiated after the dot-com bust), and an emphasis on developing people. "We now have a whole pool of talent who can lead . . . like mini CEOs and COOs. We're growing ideas but we're growing people as well," Chambers told *Fast Company*.

Chambers's message is clear. Organizations that do not have the right leadership talent in place will not survive when the economy eventually rebounds. So where does an organization begin (or continue) to develop its leadership talent? We have worked in the past with very large organizations that were putting several hundred managers through the same individual development experience. These organizations assumed that this approach would result in a well-trained group of leaders who would have a unified impact on the organization. That assumption was faulty.

The result instead was a group of individuals who knew what to do to improve their individual leadership skills but did not understand how their leadership skills could and should serve the organization as a whole. A better strategy is to create a leader development process that results in both individual *and* organizational impact.

Helping individuals improve their leadership skills can be relatively straightforward. But ensuring that those improved leadership skills have organizational impact is more complex. In our experience it requires a systematic approach that begins with the organization's strategic goals and takes into account developmental needs at both the organizational and individual levels.

Consider the following example:

A global electronics manufacturer grows quickly through acquisition. Until recently the plants it acquired operated autonomously. Because of competition, a new CEO decides to change the organizational strategy and restructure so that the plants are organized globally by market segment. In this scenario the strategic shift creates some challenges in a number of areas, including

- Maintaining clarity and effective communication of vision and mission
- Establishing a global structure that is workable both overall and for different market segments
- Coordinating once-autonomous plants and functions within those plants
- Realigning relations with internal and external customers
- Dealing in new ways with differing cultures in multiple countries

Each of these challenges has leadership implications at both the organizational and individual levels. For example, it is likely that the organizational structure will drive development of new or different coordination mechanisms and processes. At the individual level this probably means that leaders will have to develop or refine personal competencies, such as negotiation and conflict management, to name just two. If these competencies are performed well, there will be visible organizational impact.

A development process that is intended to have organizational impact will require ongoing support from key stakeholders. It is not enough for executives and others in the organization to voice support. They must model the desired individual behaviors and provide resources such as time, money, and staff to coordinate the development process and ensure that it is smoothly implemented.

FLEXIBLE SYSTEM

Keeping these points in mind, let's look at an approach that CCL calls Developing Leadership Talent (DLT). Before we examine this framework it must be pointed out that the DLT approach is not intended to be a one-size-fits-all system. Instead it provides a flexible framework for designing a development system that fits your organization's needs.

At the center of this framework, which is summarized in the graphic on page 5, is a two-level model of assessment, challenge, and support (ACS). ACS represents CCL's fundamental approach to development and grounds the entire DLT process.

Assessment. Effective development requires a baseline measure of the current state (both individual and organizational) of development. This assessment can verify or reinforce the need for development.

Challenge. Development requires moving beyond one's comfort zone; it requires a stretch.

Support. Development is much more likely to succeed if support is provided.

In short, ACS suggests that effective development requires three elements: assessment of the current skill level, identification and design of the activities that will help development occur, and the support needed to ensure sustainability of the development.

Surrounding the ACS strategy is a series of steps that we encourage you to follow to create your own organization's development strategy. Although we will discuss these steps in order, as if one follows the other in a linear fashion, they actually interact with each other in a nonlinear way. For example, you don't evaluate impact until the conclusion of an initiative but that does not mean you must wait until then to determine how and what to evaluate. In fact, you should determine the how and the what at the beginning.

Let's examine each step.

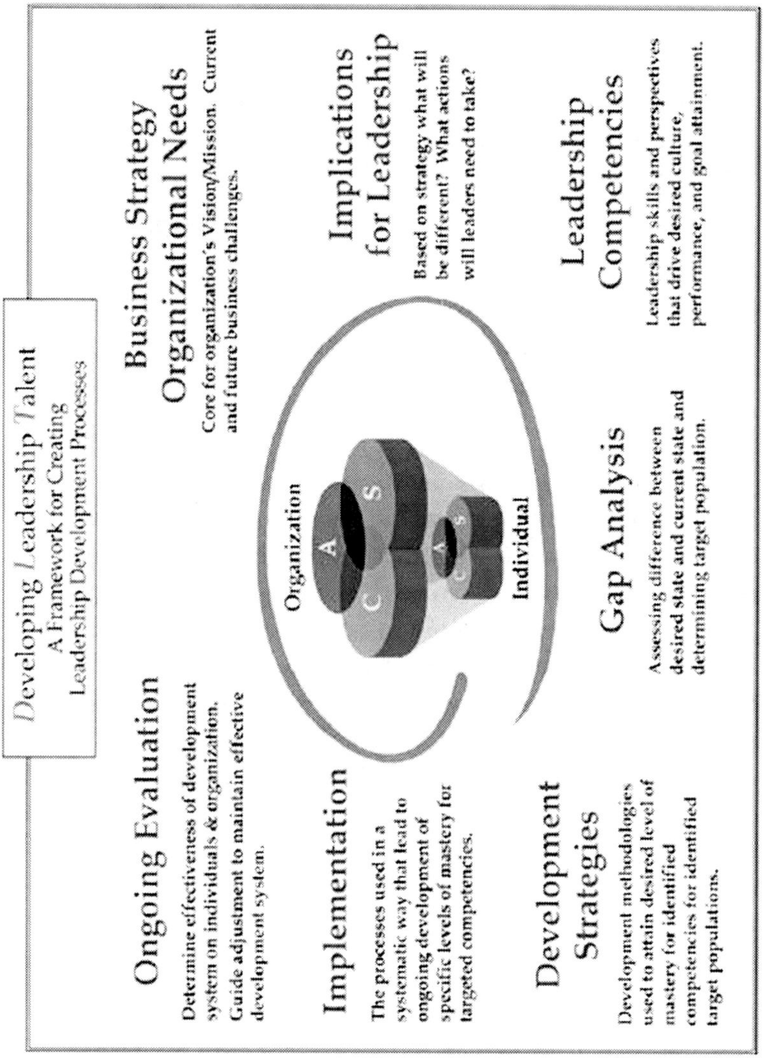

Step One

What are the key challenges facing your organization over the next planning period, generally two to five years? For a development effort to have organizational impact, it must be linked to the organization's strategy and business challenges. Here the task is to identify

- market or industry trends that are placing pressure on the organization (such as an economic downturn or disruptive technology)
- issues associated with implementing the organization's business strategy (such as resistance from within the organization)
- internal challenges (such as a recent acquisition, merger, or culture change)

Step Two

Given the challenges and issues identified in Step 1, what organizational capabilities and individual competencies must be developed or enhanced—in other words, what must the organization and its leaders do differently?

The first two steps begin to establish a foundation for the successful implementation of a development process. First, by identifying key organizational challenges and the individual competencies and organizational capabilities needed to meet these challenges, a direct link is built between the organization's needs and the development effort. This provides credibility and a way to evaluate the bottom-line impact of the development effort. Second, key stakeholders will be more likely to support the development effort because it supports accomplishing the organization's strategic goals.

Step Three

What individual leader competencies and organizational capabilities need to be refined or developed? Another way of asking this question is, if we expect our leaders to take the actions (or behave in a particular way) identified in Step 2, what specific individual skills will they need? How will those skills support necessary changes in organizational capabilities?

In the earlier example of the global electronics manufacturer, the individual competencies were negotiation and conflict management. The organizational capabilities related to items such as coordinating once-autonomous plants and functions within those plants and realigning relations with internal and external customers.

Stakeholders also may play a role in deciding on the competencies and capabilities to be developed. Even if stakeholders are not involved in detailed discussions, it often is useful to review with them and get their support by linking all your work during this step back to the strategic goals.

Step Four

The focus here is on determining the specific target populations for development. Not everyone must or can become proficient in a particular competency or competency set. Consequently, it is important to identify the skill level to be developed. Does the individual need only rudimentary skills, or must that person become an expert?

It is also important to prioritize the development of the target groups. Who goes first? Why? Will that first effort be evaluated before another group participates in a development process?

Step Five

What methodologies will be used to build organizational capability and individual competency? Organizations have a wide range of methodologies to choose from, including action-learning projects, cross-functional projects and teams, developmental job assignments, coaching, mentoring, 360-degree feedback, assessment centers, and formal training programs.

The methodologies you choose must facilitate closing the gap between current and desired levels of skill and capability. Defining that gap is important because it will help guide the design and evaluation of your initiative. It is also helpful at this point to determine what type of follow-up or application activities participants must engage in.

Step 5 is also where various organizational constraints should be considered. These constraints may include time, money, facility use, technologies and traditions already in place, administrative support, and procurement requirements.

For example, the designer may find himself or herself losing credibility if he or she pushes vigorously for a three-day leadership program when company practice supports one day or less. In our experience it is better to propose an acceptable solution—even if it is not optimal—and then help organizational practice evolve toward the optimal. Here again, key stakeholders can play an important role.

The kinds of development methods and activities that have worked well in the past can also influence current choices. It will be useful to know what worked and why. As noted earlier, you almost certainly will need to explain how the initiative you are proposing builds on an earlier development initiative.

It's equally important to know what was not successful and why. Organizational memories are long. We have worked with organizations where a failure paralyzed leadership development efforts for years after—such efforts became too risky. If you know this has happened in your organization, you may be able to identify a less risky work-around and build from there.

Finally, as noted earlier, even though evaluation is not done until after implementation, the focus and approach to evaluation should be determined before implementation and then modified as needed. Here are some questions you should consider:

- How will you know when the development gap you have identified has been closed? Items to consider include the specific goals, objectives, and outcomes you are trying to achieve; the kind of information (qualitative or quantitative) you will need to demonstrate that the goals, objectives, and outcomes have been met; and how best to design the initiative to ensure you can get that information.

- What processes do you have in place for determining and measuring the impact of the leadership development initiative on both individuals and the organization?
- How will you evaluate the effectiveness of the various components of the leadership development initiative (content, learning methodology, classroom training, online training, and faculty)?
- How will you collect enough information to inform yourself and important stakeholders about future leadership development initiatives?

Step Six

This step involves the implementation of the development strategy and builds directly on the types of decisions just discussed. Implementation is more than simply the logistics of putting people through the development process. It is also about maintaining organizational support for the development process.

If you have involved key stakeholders in the creation of the development process, they will be more likely to support the effort and to help build acceptance among managers and other employees throughout the organization. They also will be more likely to understand the resource requirements of the initiative and to provide support for obtaining these resources. For example, depending on the size and complexity of the effort, you may need a project manager, use of certain facilities, and acquisition of copyrighted materials, among other things.

Step Seven

This is the formal evaluation of your initiative. Evaluation tells you whether the development process has had the desired impact on individuals and the organization. It can also help you determine how well the development methodology or methodologies worked and how to be more effective in the future. As noted earlier, to be effective, evaluation must be considered from the beginning of an initiative. The objectives on which the design is based should also be evaluated.

STRATEGIC GOALS

Leadership development can and should have both individual and organizational impact. To accomplish both, we recommend beginning with an organization's strategic business goals and assessing current capabilities against future needs: in other words, does the organization have the talent it needs to accomplish its strategic goals?

A leadership development initiative requires effective management within the organization. Building and maintaining support among key stakeholders can be very important for both encouraging broader organizational support and acquiring necessary resources. Knowing what has worked and not worked in the past and what may or may not be possible in your organization is also essential. That information will often help you to define what will be addressed in your initiative and how.

Engaging and Developing Is Key to the Challenge

Robin Athey and Robert Burnside

Despite the fact that there are millions of unemployed people in the United States, there remains an acute shortage of talent that is transforming today's business world. Top-level talent is scarce and becoming even more so because of two factors: the retirement of baby boomers and a growing skills gap.

The first members of the baby boom generation have hit their mid-sixties, and the proportion of the workforce made up of people fifty or older has snowballed and will continue to do so. What's more, the nation's education system is not keeping pace with the increasing complexity of business and technology. Only 70 percent of U.S. public high school students graduate on time, and only 32 percent leave high school qualified to attend a four-year college.

Consequently, companies that want to excel must be able to not only attract and retain talented employees but also engage these workers as never before. Jobs that have become increasingly dynamic will require companies to train and develop employees simply to keep pace with change. At the same time, individuals need to be afforded greater flexibility in their career paths, and organizations need to reap greater flexibility from employees.

Companies traditionally have responded to tightening labor markets by launching recruitment bidding wars, but we challenge this thinking. Even the best recruitment tactics will not be enough to combat today's talent challenge. High compensation packages and bonuses are easily matched by competitors. Instead, a more discerning response is required.

This article outlines the major factors precipitating today's talent challenge, a few assumptions about effective ways to rethink approaches to that challenge, and methods companies can use to address today's diminishing talent pipeline.

SUPPLY AND DEMAND

What is the talent challenge? Primarily, it is the rising demand for capable performers and the dwindling supply of such employees. The approximately seventy-six million baby boomers in the United States (those born between 1946 and 1963) are beginning to retire in great numbers. The sixty-six million U.S. members of Generation X (those born between 1965 and 1983) and even the seventy-five million U.S. members of Generation Y (or Millennials, those born between 1984 and 2002) will not be enough to fill the gap.

Paralleling this development is a lack of engagement in the education system among new-generation students. In many ways, the current high school system has not kept pace and is not teaching tomorrow's workforce how to apply logic and problem solving in order to tackle the complex challenges of our fast-changing world. One result is that students are becoming disinterested in or are dropping out of high school, compounding the talent shortage. Consider these statistics: 70 percent of public high school students graduate on time, yet 85 percent of jobs require education beyond high school, 60 percent of new jobs in this century will require skills possessed by only 20 percent of the current workforce, and 79 percent of companies will see a significant shortage in the talent pipeline (40 percent of companies say this is already an acute problem).

A second reason for today's talent challenge is employee churn and growing discontent. Satisfaction levels among all workers, regardless of age, income, or location, have been in decline for two decades. Less than half of American workers are satisfied with their jobs, down from 61 percent twenty years ago. And less than 39 percent of workers under the age of twenty-five are satisfied with their jobs.

A third reason for the talent challenge is the increasing complexity of today's jobs. Globalization, technological advancement, and information overload complicate today's work environment. With the reach provided by modern information technology, people are globally connected 24–7, receiving nonstop information and a barrage of cognitive demands. One study found that the average employee switches tasks every three minutes, is interrupted every two minutes, and has a maximum focus period of twelve minutes. This constant switching saps creativity, impedes decision making, and weakens performance.

With fewer bodies, growing job dissatisfaction, and increasing job complexity, there is a clear need for organizations and their leaders to engage people as never before in order to strengthen their capacity to attract and retain talented people.

In seeking approaches to engage today's workforce, three assumptions can be made. One is that employees work for more than a paycheck. They seek jobs that challenge them to learn and grow. Employees offer their best when they feel they can make meaningful contributions toward a vision with purpose and backed by a clear strategy.

A second assumption is that new strategies are required to meet these employee desires. The traditional response to talent shortages has been to *acquire* and *retain* people—that is, to recruit them and keep them "in their seats." Such strategies focus on metrics that are important to an organization. To truly engage people, however, talent strategies must focus on what matters most to employees—their development—in ways that promote learning and growth, their deployment into roles they care about, and their connection to the people and things that help them do their best work. Not surprisingly, organizations that create experiences that spark people's fullest capabilities attract and retain—and create—the best talent.

A third assumption is that learning must be knitted into the fabric of work. Such learning will include both formal interventions (classroom programs, online courses, and executive coaching) and workplace learning (mentoring, expert networks, and collaborative spaces).

EIGHT APPROACHES

How, then, can organizations start meeting the growing talent challenge, short of radically restructuring their business career-track models? As a starting point, here are eight practical approaches that companies can employ right away.

Be strategic about bringing on new employees. A new employee's first experience shouldn't be about orientation courses and human resource manuals. It should be about connections. It takes about six months to socialize new hires. Leaders can accelerate the process and foster loyalty by connecting new hires with experienced "buddies" and mentors. The tacit knowledge that emerges from these interactions can convey values in much more compelling ways than bullet points or mission statements can. It is also useful to encourage recruits to observe and ask questions about policy and processes, rather than jump into the old ways of doing things.

Match people to roles that suit their strengths and capabilities. Each individual is capable of doing many things, but people are more likely to put forth their best efforts in roles they love performing rather than in roles where they are asked to perform only the things they're skilled in. To help them realize these best efforts, many leading organizations provide internal support centers and coaching to help employees navigate their careers. These companies also give employees the flexibility to try out different roles in order to find their niche. This is an ongoing process that benefits both employees and companies: as people's capabilities and interests shift during their careers, companies' needs also shift.

Encourage productive conversations. Conversations shape relationships, and relationships are the number one reason why people stay or go. Moreover, work gets done through conversations, and conversations are the primary source of learning. More than 70 percent of what people know comes through informal interactions with others. Consequently, leaders at all levels must look closely at opportunities for conversations—both theirs and others'—in situations such as meetings, day-to-day interactions, and performance reviews. Many organizations benefit by becoming more intentional about conversations—for instance, encouraging ongoing performance dialogues instead of highly stressful annual or semiannual reviews. Some organizations encourage *peer assists* by bringing together seasoned practitioners and less-experienced team members in one- or two-day knowledge-sharing sessions. Such interactions build morale in junior employees because the opportunity to work with senior colleagues is a form of recognition.

Explore existing and emerging collaborative tools and approaches. A number of new technologies and methods have been developed to make communication and collaboration more efficient. One focus is e-mail. Because roughly 60 percent of e-mail is spam and only 8 percent is truly important, establishing best practices for e-mail can significantly improve efficiency. New online media also can be powerful tools when used responsibly. Blogs are opening a new level of knowledge sharing and dialogue, and wikis—Web sites that allow users to add and edit content collectively—are enabling coworkers to collaborate in real time. However, the focus here must always be on the quality of the collaboration, not just on the tools that enable the collaboration.

Cultivate strategic communities. Communities have always existed in organizations, but now technology allows people to connect in new ways that promote learning and innovation. Companies can provide forums where employees can exchange ideas and work through issues of complexity and change. These communities also serve as magnets for commitment. Employees considering departing a company may think twice about leaving colleagues who have shared interests and experiences. Communities have the potential to foster an esprit de corps and a mind-set of innovative thinking that teams operating in traditional hierarchies cannot easily achieve.

Stimulate networks of high-quality relationships. Informal social networks also engage employees in ways that promote learning and growth. One approach begins with social-network analysis—a map of relationships that provides an X-ray of the way projects are completed. Once they understand the ways that people connect, collaborate, and share knowledge, managers can create conditions that lead to optimal individual and organizational performance.

Design physical workspaces to foster connections. Workplace designs that offer dedicated spaces for formal collaboration, quiet places to concentrate, and informal areas to relax and brainstorm are critical for effective communication and collaboration. When workers are more than thirty yards apart, interaction falls off precipitously. The design of a space should reflect intent. When collaboration is important, open workspaces can be more effective than closed ones because conversations spill over and informal networking occurs that might not otherwise.

Build an organizational cushion of time and space. As the pace of business speeds up and decisions become more complex, employees need time and space to learn, reflect, and produce work with tangible results. What are leading organizations doing? Some allow workers to pursue professional projects of personal interest. Others offer employees the flexibility to choose work locations and methods that match their natural rhythms. No matter the approach, leaders must act as role models for the practices they advocate and be mindful of the messages they send. Leaders who glorify emergencies and view long hours as noble and heroic can trigger stress and family conflicts that hurt performance.

LOOK WITHIN

In coming years, most companies will have to rethink their talent strategies. In addition to addressing shifting demographics, improving the performance of critical employees directly improves organizational performance. Organizations should look within for the critical skills required to execute the company's most important jobs. By developing, deploying, and connecting these people the right way, leaders can raise individuals' performances—and the performance of the entire organization.

How to Put Your Finger on the High Potentials

David Berke

In any organization there are individuals who are considered to be the likely future leaders of the organization—in other words, to have high potential for leadership. Developing and retaining these high-potential individuals is crucial to an organization's long-term success. But before high potentials can be developed and retained they must be identified.

The process of identifying high potentials might appear to be obvious and simple—you merely determine which individuals are most intelligent and perform best, right? But identifying high potentials—and just as important, the people who should no longer be considered high potentials—involves looking at more than just performance and IQ. And an organization's ability to conduct this identification process successfully has an enormous impact on the effectiveness of its succession planning.

Typically, people identified as high potentials are viewed as being capable of advancing two or more levels up from their current positions. In some cases the definition is even narrower, focusing only on those who are believed to have the potential to make it to the very top level of the organization.

Such definitions are both too general and too limiting—too general because they provide little specific guidance for selecting high potentials, and too limiting because they contain an implicit or sometimes explicit assumption that being high potential means being capable of filling a position at the highest rungs of the organization.

In fact, for a variety of reasons, few people will ever have an opportunity to lead a company or even a large segment of a company. Many people simply don't want to, and of those who do, few can do the job effectively. There are many examples of people who performed well in a specialty area or function but were unable to make a successful transition to top management.

But people who don't have the desire or ability to make it to the top can still contribute significant value to the organization. To survive and thrive, organizations need a seasoned cadre of professionals and high performers. At earlier points in their careers, many of these people probably were considered high potentials, but they reached the limits of their upward movement. However, the fact that these people will not move into senior corporate management does not necessarily mean that their status as high potentials should end—they still could be considered for important positions in specialty areas or functions. In other words, there can be—and should be—different types of high potentials.

NO GUARANTEES

As noted earlier, intelligence and performance may seem to be the most obvious and dependable indicators of high potential. However, the evidence is that although high IQ and performance usually get people noticed, they do not guarantee success.

In a 2002 article in *The New Yorker*, staff writer Malcolm Gladwell states that research has found almost no link between IQ and job performance. The correlation between IQ and occupational success, he writes, is between 0.2 and 0.3—a negligible connection at best. (He suggests that a strong correlation would be 0.7 or higher.) Gladwell quoted Richard Wagner, a psychologist at Florida State University: "What IQ doesn't pick up is effectiveness at common-sense sorts of things, especially in working with people. In terms of how we evaluate schooling, everything is about working by yourself. If you work with someone else, it's called cheating. Once you get out in the real world, everything you do involves working with people."

Building and expanding on this idea, Michael M. Lombardo and Robert W. Eichinger, in their book *The Leadership*

Machine: Architecture to Develop Leaders for Any Future (Lominger International, 2006), point out that if identifying high potentials were merely a matter of assessing intelligence, organizations that hire only college graduates with grade point averages of 3.5 or higher and with IQs of 120 or above would never experience a talent shortage or a lack of bench strength for key management and leadership roles. And yet most companies with such hiring policies do have these problems. Lombardo and Eichinger write that although IQ is valuable as an indicator of analytical skill and the ability to acquire new technical knowledge, it is not connected with the ability to acquire new behavior—to be *learning agile.*

Lombardo and Eichinger suggest that it is these learning agile people, who can continually learn from experience to do something new or different, who are most likely to be an organization's true high potentials. But because intelligence is far easier to assess than is learning agility, those in an organization who are responsible for identifying high potentials tend to depend too much on judgments of intelligence.

Just as intelligence provides no guarantee of success in top leadership positions, neither do high performance and extensive experience in meeting job requirements that are different—usually less complex—from the requirements at the top of an organization. People who have performed well over time in a specific function probably have a great deal of potential for taking a position one or two levels up in their specialty area, where they will mostly be doing more of the same. But this does not mean they are able to learn new functions and effectively perform a variety of assignments. Again, a key element among high potentials is the ability to learn continuously and adapt to new challenges and unfamiliar circumstances.

ROADBLOCKS

No selection process is ever free of bias, and the identification of high potentials is no exception, even if the process is rigorous.

There will always be people who should be considered for high-potential status but will be excluded for reasons that have little to do with their abilities or their learning agility.

If an individual's personality does not "fit" with that of his or her peers or boss—in other words, if the person consistently views and responds to events differently from the way other members of the group do—it can mark the individual as an outsider and substantially reduce his or her chances of leading the group effectively and therefore of being perceived as a high potential.

A company's industry type and the organizational culture that emerges from it can also have an effect on who will or will not be identified as high potentials and continue on to top leadership positions. Research shows that in companies in highly concentrated industries with predictable, well-defined competition, a premium is placed on using a fairly bounded set of analytical and problem-solving routines; in companies in highly distinct, high-growth industries, the opposite appears to be the case. So a person's chances of being identified as a high potential and avoiding derailment can largely depend on whether his or her analytical and problem-solving styles match up with those that prevail in the industry. Here, being learning agile can take on specific requirements and limitations.

Bias according to race and gender still exists, of course, although the playing field has been leveled considerably in the past thirty years. At a more subtle level, executives responsible for identifying high potentials sometimes are simply unwilling to change their minds about or to consider data that contradict their previously formed opinions of an individual. Sometimes a person just does not have the right educational background—scientists, for example, often want to be managed only by other scientists. Or perhaps a person's alma mater is not considered elite enough.

GOING DEEP

What do companies do after tentatively identifying those who might be high potentials? Typically, a competency model specifically designed for the company is used as the basis for assessments that go beyond the annual performance review and anecdotal data gathered by the human resource department. Such assessments may include a multi-rater feedback instrument derived from the competency model as well as other types of instruments and measures of personality. Some companies also use outside assessment centers, where candidates participate in exercises that simulate actual leadership situations in the organization. Assessment centers are usually very effective but can be expensive.

In-depth assessments can provide data that are highly useful in identifying high potentials. These data also may justify expenditures on the development of high potentials, costs that often constitute a large percentage of a company's development budget. But such assessments are not a silver bullet; applying a current competency model to future challenges, for instance, can be problematic.

The pencil-and-paper assessments are more suited for identifying high potentials at the lower levels of an organization than at the higher levels. Positions at higher levels often involve an exponential increase in scope and complexity—the higher one goes, the more complex are the elements to be learned. So the ability to continually learn and adapt, although necessary, is not sufficient. This is where IQ becomes an important factor, as do emotional intelligence and a range of skills including negotiation, dealing with ambiguity, developing others, and managing conflict.

For this reason the assessments should be augmented by the observations of several raters. (This applies especially to the higher levels but also to the lower levels.) The raters might include the person's immediate supervisor, the manager at the next level up, and a human resource representative. It's not a good idea to depend solely on the evaluation of the person's immediate supervisor, whose perspective may be too limited. It's also unrealistic to expect a high-potential employee to perform a specific function better than a seasoned professional in that specialty does.

At the higher levels the CEO and executive management team can act as the assessors. This works best when the succession planning process has been centralized, the talent in question is perceived as "belonging" to the organization rather than to a specific department, the top executives have made the effort and taken the time to work out criteria for assessment, and the CEO does not play favorites or allow others to.

EXPANDING THE POOL

As mentioned earlier, organizations are well advised to not confine their lists of high potentials to those people capable of ascending to CEO or another top-rung position. In fact, it can be argued that talent pools and pipelines should be developed at many organizational levels and that they should feed both laterally and upward. There are a number of reasons for this.

- There are no guarantees about who can or will make it to the top.
- When there is a promotion from one level to another, the position vacated at the lower level needs to be filled.
- Critical positions—not just in management but also technical jobs—exist throughout an organization. A sudden departure in one of these less-visible positions can be damaging unless there is a pool of qualified candidates ready to be considered for the job.
- When business conditions change, business strategy often changes along with them. Someone who appeared to be the right candidate under a previous strategy may no longer be the right candidate under the new strategy.
- Finally, it's important to be able to consider more than one person to fill a position. It's advisable to develop at least three people for each position. This not only allows

for turnover and changes in job requirements but also provides diversity in the candidate pool.

FULL DISCLOSURE?

Once an organization compiles a list of high potentials, the question arises whether the list should be made public. Arguments can be made on both sides.

One of the dangers of making the list public is that people may remain on the list even after it becomes apparent that they are no longer learning or growing more quickly than their peers. But those who put an individual on the list are often hesitant to remove that person from the list, not only because they are unwilling to admit they were wrong but also because of the significant negative ramifications that withdrawal from the list can have for the individual's career and relationships with others in the organization.

In addition, when high potentials are on a public list, they may begin to believe they are exempt from many of the rules of behavior that apply to others, and will act accordingly. To protect themselves and their high-potential status, they may avoid necessary risks or act in a conservative way that hinders their ability to learn and grow. Also, unless the organization is very careful about explaining what it means to be a high potential, people on a public list may develop incorrect assumptions.

There are also some good reasons for making the list public. For instance, it can facilitate discussions with the high potentials about development and encourage them to take on developmental assignments. Also, when the process of identifying and developing high potentials is open, it gains credibility among employees.

Perhaps the most important point for those responsible for identifying and developing high potentials to keep in mind is that there are high potentials in all parts of an organization. Not all of them are capable of rising to CEO, but many can perform well in their specific functions and specialties if the development pipeline is opened to them as well.

Building the Pipeline: Leadership Succession Is a Key Challenge

Anjali Hazarika

In times of uncertainty, turbulence, and intense competition like these, companies now more than ever need to focus on strengthening their pipelines of talent and ensuring successful leadership transition. The example of a large hydrocarbon exploration and production company in India shows how to tackle the challenge.

Strategy, growth, and use of technology are just a few of the significant factors that determine the success and effectiveness of any organization, but organizations would not get very far in achieving these goals if they didn't have capable and motivated leaders to carry them out. It goes without saying that the depth and quality of an organization's leadership are the most important determinants of the organization's future, and that especially in uncertain and turbulent times such as these, companies need to focus on building their pipelines of talent and ensuring successful leadership transition. Leadership transition can be viewed as a potential roadblock, but if companies approach it in the right way it can offer valuable opportunities for both the organization and individual leaders.

A paradigm that models how companies can go about meeting the challenges of managing leadership succession and strengthening their leadership pipelines can be found in Oil India Limited (OIL), a large hydrocarbon exploration and production company in India under the administrative control of the Indian government's Ministry of Petroleum and Natural Gas. OIL is engaged in the exploration, development, and production of crude oil and natural gas; the transportation of crude oil; and the production of liquid petroleum gas. It is the pioneer in the exploration and production of hydrocarbons in India.

The issues of managing leadership succession and building the talent pipeline became critical for OIL in 2007, when the

company realized that thirty-five of its senior executives—general managers and deputy general managers—would retire by 2010. If not addressed urgently, this exodus of top leaders would create a leadership crisis. How could the company keep the leadership pipeline filled with capable leaders to succeed the current top management team? OIL clearly recognized that leadership effectiveness and succession management are key to driving outstanding business performance and competitiveness. It viewed the lack of qualified leadership talent in the pipeline as its most significant constraint on growth. OIL's business strategy was to invest in high-growth opportunities overseas and to become a global player, so what kind of leaders would it need to follow that strategy? The company decided that it would need leaders who could be held accountable for cultivating others, diagnosing gaps in execution and capability, and redirecting manpower resources to address business strategies. It also knew that its top leadership team would need feedback and insight into where it had succeeded in building the talent pipeline and where there were potential risks. The company settled on applying a *measurement mind-set* to the often inexact process of developing the next generation of leaders.

OIL decided to conduct a thorough diagnostic assessment of its top twenty-six executives (with the required amount of tenure) to identify areas of leadership competency development and then offer customized leadership development models that would address the specific needs of the senior executives in relation to their critical roles in the organization.

FOUR FACTORS

To define talent management and address areas such as succession planning, competency model development, and talent gap analysis, OIL decided to partner with the Hay Group, a global management consulting firm that works with organizations to develop talent and organize people to be more effective and motivated to perform to their full potential. The Hay Group gathers and applies deeply researched global data on competency models and leadership effectiveness. Its work is based on seminal research by David McClelland, an American psychological theorist noted for his work from the 1950s until the 1990s on achievement motivation and consciousness.

Through extensive research conducted at Harvard and Boston Universities, four key factors have been identified and linked directly with superior individual and organizational performance: organizational climate, leadership styles, individual competencies, and job requirements.

Organizational climate. Of the four key variables, climate has the greatest impact on individual and organizational performance. The more positively employees perceive their climate, the greater the effort they put into their jobs and the more they commit themselves to achieving targets, managing crises, and reducing costs. In a healthy climate, people are encouraged to perform to high standards, are developed to take on more responsibility, are recognized and rewarded for outstanding contributions, and take pride in individual and group accomplishments. A healthy climate leads to increased revenue growth, efficiency, and profitability. Organizational climate is largely determined by leadership styles.

Leadership styles. Styles refer to patterns of behavior a leader uses across the full range of management situations. This is the variable that has the most impact on organizational climate. The breadth of a leader's repertoire of styles determines his or her effectiveness. Leaders prefer to use styles that are most natural to them and therefore they may limit themselves to using only those styles. What feels natural is largely determined by a leader's individual competencies.

Individual competencies. Competencies include the skills, knowledge, self-image, and values a manager brings to the job. The strongest characteristic that affects individual behavior is motivation. Understanding why they are naturally inclined to behave in certain ways allows managers to predict, monitor, and manage their behavior. The ability to consciously choose an appropriate behavior improves leadership effectiveness and enhances organizational climate and performance. But because each job is different, different competencies are required to do different jobs.

Competencies generate behaviors that get better results more consistently across a broad range of managerial situations. They are more than the basic threshold capabilities such as IQ or technical skills.

Job requirements. In developing effective management practices, an analysis of the objective requirements of the job is as important as the assessment of individual leadership styles and competencies. Understanding the difference between job requirements and what people find naturally satisfying explains why managers perform well in some aspects of their job and why they find some aspects frustrating.

SETTING A FRAMEWORK

The philosophy embodied in the four factors linked with superior individual and organizational performance provided the context for OIL's rigorous and focused assessment of leadership talent. Once convinced that this methodology was robust, OIL launched its initiative, called Project Competence.

Project Competence was envisaged as a large-scale, complex project. OIL knew that an effective competency framework would have to incorporate an accurate understanding of the firm's strategic business context and current and future business challenges. Interviews were set up with the chairman, the managing director, and other directors and senior executives with critical roles. These dialogues enabled OIL to identify the future leadership capabilities that were required and to confirm these capabilities through presentation to and discussion with the executive team. This process also ensured the involvement of the executive team and enabled it to set direction, create alignment, and seek commitment. A competency framework was then created from these findings.

Next, after detailed analysis of the job descriptions of the twenty-six executives mentioned earlier, general managers and deputy general managers who were likely to succeed the soon-to-retire leaders, a talent matrix was developed for each role and a competency questionnaire was developed. The questionnaire encompassed sixteen competencies, including committed leadership, adaptability, development of others, ability to influence others, skill in partnering, and organizational awareness. The executives were then tested through a variety of 360-degree feedback instruments—including the competency questionnaire, an inventory of leadership styles, and an organizational climate survey—that were completed by the executives' bosses, peers, and direct reports. Their competencies, as judged by these instruments, then were compared with the competency framework containing the organization's most critical traits for highly effective leaders.

The twenty-six executives were also extensively interviewed using the behavioral event interview method. They were asked for specific examples of past behaviors that related to the competencies required to do a job well—the principle being that the best predictor of future performance is past performance in similar circumstances. The executives were also given comprehensive feedback on the reports generated by all the instruments. The aggregate results of the survey were presented to the executive team, the twenty-six executives, and their managers.

Developing self-awareness is the first step toward leadership development. The talent review led to useful conversations with the twenty-six executives that had never taken place before and that helped begin the process of shifting beliefs and values concerning talent management issues in the company. The talent review indicated certain common areas of development, certain individual development needs specific to function or location, and certain organizational climate issues that required urgent attention. OIL decided to tackle these issues one by one.

CHANGED SCENARIO

OIL's strategic business context has changed considerably in recent years. It has taken on an increasingly global presence, with operations in seven countries outside India. This expanded business scenario has created a need for increased development in such areas as commercial business savvy and strategic orientation; negotiation, power, influence, and relationship skills and management; and leadership style repertoire. OIL decided to address this need with two independent leadership development programs provided by Duke Corporate Education, a collaboration of the Fuqua School of Business at Duke University, the London School of Economics, and the Indian Institute of Management (IIM) in Ahmedabad. Duke Corporate Education is perennially ranked No. 1 by *BusinessWeek* and the *Financial Times* in the field of customized corporate education. Both programs were highly customized and included an action-learning component. The first five-day program was delivered in June 2008 at IIM in Ahmedabad, and the second took place in Calcutta in July 2008.

Skill in managing interpersonal relationships may sometimes be derided as a "soft skill," but research has shown it to be one of the main differentiating factors in leadership success. Every effort was made in the two programs to facilitate the application of new learning in the context of people's work situations. To that end the participants were given two assignments over a period of four months. One was a group action-learning project and the other was an individual assignment to groom at least two successors.

Leadership development is a shared responsibility. Its building blocks are assessment, challenge, and support. Thus the talent review was only the first piece—the assessment. To practice new leadership behaviors the twenty-six executives needed some challenge in their work assignments and also support from their bosses—they could not be expected to be change agents without such support. It was also important to ensure that the degree of assessment and challenge was such that the participants would be inspired rather than unmotivated to address the issues discovered through the organizational climate survey.

For that to happen the bosses also needed to understand how their leadership styles and individual characteristics affected organizational climate and how an improved climate can lead to superior organizational performance. So they also were tested through the competency questionnaire, the inventory of leadership styles, and the organizational climate survey, along with a self-reported picture-story exercise and a questionnaire on personal values. An analysis of the resulting data culminated in a three-day leadership development workshop followed by a one-day extended leadership team workshop.

These workshops enabled the bosses to set up meaningful dialogues with the twenty-six executives regarding individual development plans. Learning new leadership behaviors requires breaking old habits. It also requires an individualized approach, motivation to change, practice, and feedback from the boss. The dialogues, conducted once every two months, gave the twenty-six executives an opportunity to cover new information and new perspectives, interact with their bosses, solicit specific advice, and continue on a dynamic growth path.

GETTING BETTER

OIL's organizational climate survey revealed that the company needed to work on certain critical dimensions of the climate. Climate affects organizational performance through its influence on employee motivation. High-performing organizations have identified the specific and measurable climate dimensions that consistently demonstrate the greatest impact on individual and organizational performance. These dimensions are *flexibility, responsibility, standards, rewards and recognition, role clarity,* and *team commitment*. It is evident that these climate dimensions are also important leadership functions. How could these elements serve OIL's business strategy?

Changing the Leadership Paradigm

In order to build an effective, functional leadership pipeline a company has to move from a CEO-dependent culture to a more interdependent culture to support business objectives, goals, and strategies that require coordinated actions across functions, locations, and regions. This calls for developing multiple leaders to take on leadership roles at multiple levels and for thinking differently about leadership. Think of a trapeze artist balancing himself on a tightrope while carrying two other people on his shoulders. That is what a CEO feels like as he tries to maintain a precarious balance while carrying his direct reports on his shoulders and being totally answerable and accountable for the business results. In the past it has often been assumed that only a CEO in a position of total authority can be responsible for leadership. But what if she had the support of groomed successors who take collective responsibility for corporate performance? How much easier would it be to address business issues?

In that case it is the CEO who is carried on the shoulders of three or more able members of the executive team. It is a paradigm shift from having a single point of leadership to having collective leadership, from investing in only one talented individual, who represents the company as a champion responsible for winning every game, to developing many champions, whose focus is on increasing the overall chances of winning. This shift of focus from an individual, single point leadership to a leadership culture that is conducive to the effective development of other leaders can significantly improve organizational performance.

OIL recognized that it had room for improvement in four of the main climate dimensions and in two subdimensions. It set up six task teams on role clarity, standards, autonomy and risk taking, innovation, rewards and recognition, and team commitment. The key questions in determining the presence or absence of role clarity are whether employees know how they contribute to the organization's mission and whether policies, procedures, and lines of authority are clearly articulated and understood. The keys to standards are setting challenging and attainable goals and determining whether employees place importance on doing their best. Autonomy and risk taking are a subdimension of responsibility and involve delegating important tasks to employees and encouraging employees to take calculated risks. Innovation is a subdimension of flexibility and involves the extent to which people are free to innovate without unreasonable constraints. The dimension of rewards and recognition is about determining how rewards are tied to performance. Team commitment reflects the degree of feelings of trust and pride in the organization.

Each task team was assigned a functional director who was requested to champion the team by further enrolling cross-functional members. The task teams met once a month with the conviction that their work would significantly improve the four main climate dimensions and two subdimensions.

OIL's efforts to better manage its leadership succession and strengthen its leadership pipeline are ongoing, but there is strong evidence that the company's systematic approach is working.

STAYING AHEAD

In the final analysis, no matter how sophisticated your technology, how effective your strategy, or how efficient your processes, sooner or later a competitor will duplicate your achievement. This is true whether you compete in a single country or around the world. Regardless of your size a competitor is always aiming at you. The only way to stay ahead in this never-ending race is to build on the leadership ability of your people. That is one competitive advantage that can never be duplicated.

Learning a Lesson in Executive Selection

Robert Hogan and Robert B. Kaiser

The English philosopher Gilbert Ryle famously distinguished between two forms of knowing. The first involves knowing *that* something is the case and concerns factual knowledge; the second involves knowing *how* to do something and concerns procedural knowledge.

Organizational psychologists know that there is a right way and a wrong way to choose people who can perform well in specific jobs. Moreover, there is no difference, in principle, between the method for choosing good CEOs and the method for choosing good janitors—although the consequences of choosing a bad CEO are much more severe than the consequences of choosing a bad janitor. However, tested knowledge and proven methods for making good selection decisions are all but ignored when it comes to how CEOs are hired.

A friend of ours, an expert in employee selection, consulted with a franchise in the National Basketball Association. To his dismay they hired player after player based on technical ability, and each of these players was subsequently released—at great cost—for reasons of bad conduct. We asked our friend why the franchise owners ignored his hiring advice, and he said, "There is so much money and ego involved in these decisions that no one cares what I think." Much the same sentiment seems to apply in the process of selecting CEOs. CCL's research on executive selection confirms that little rigor is used when appointing top leaders.

CEO selection is prone to three recurring problems.

First, CEOs are invariably chosen by boards of directors, and board politics are a major factor driving the hiring decision. Jeffrey Sonnenfeld, founder of the Chief Executive Leadership

Institute at the Yale School of Management, once observed that when boards choose CEOs, the process resembles a junior high school class election.

Second, CEOs are usually chosen based on their demonstrated technical abilities. They are invariably very good at some aspect of business—they have a well-honed specialty of some sort that creates an aura of expertise. But they are rarely chosen on the basis of a demonstrated talent for leadership. This is consistent with the widespread popular belief that leadership is a function of circumstances, that if people are in charge of something, they are by definition leaders.

Finally, CEOs are often chosen based on their perceived ability to handle a single, narrowly defined issue. In the case of Hewlett-Packard, for example, one powerful member of the board wanted a new CEO who could consummate a merger with Compaq. So HP brought in Carly Fiorina. She was hired for the express purpose of buying Compaq, and no consideration was given to her prior performance as a leader. This proved to be a big mistake.

RAPID RISE

The case of Stanley O'Neal, former CEO and chairman of Merrill Lynch and a former board member of General Motors, exemplifies several important themes in CEO selection, performance, and leadership.

O'Neal was born in rural Alabama to a farming family. As a teenager, he started work on a General Motors assembly line in Atlanta, where he was identified as having high potential. GM sent him on scholarship to the General Motors Institute and then Harvard Business School, where he completed an M.B.A. degree in 1978. He returned to GM as an analyst, and three years later was a director in the treasury division. He joined Merrill Lynch in 1986 and advanced quickly, running the leveraged finance division in the early 1990s. After serving as global head of capital markets and co-head of the corporate and institutional client group, jobs in which he gained a reputation for hard-nosed analytical skill, he served as CFO from 1998 to 2000. This remarkably rapid rise suggests that O'Neal is smart, ambitious, and talented at organizational advancement, but says nothing about his leadership ability.

Meanwhile, the CEO of Merrill Lynch, David Komansky, who was widely popular among the company's employees, began losing favor with the board, in part because other competitors seemed to be growing more rapidly and in part because he developed a reputation for a loose and perhaps too collegial management style. Merrill Lynch was known to accept lower profit margins in order to pay and retain veteran employees. Industry watchers believe that the board forced Komansky to appoint O'Neal as president and heir apparent in 2001. In 2002, Komansky retired, and O'Neal became CEO and chairman—the first African American to run a major Wall Street firm. He pushed his staff to match industry leader Goldman Sachs and began buying mortgages to package into securities. Experts say O'Neal did not understand risk management, and further note that neither the Merrill Lynch board nor the executive team included anyone with deep knowledge of subprime mortgages who could properly evaluate the soundness of these substantial bets. At the same time, Goldman Sachs and JPMorgan Chase were reducing their investments in the mortgage securities business.

O'Neal's mandate from the board was to shake things up, which in part would require overhauling Merrill Lynch's legendary supportive culture, referred to as "Mother Merrill." O'Neal moved quickly, cutting 25,000 employees (a third of the total workforce) and nineteen top executives, most of whom were his potential rivals. He did this, according to National Public Radio, with "ruthless efficiency." He aroused substantial resentment by firing popular managers who had been friendly with Komansky, and he tried to change the culture from one of collegiality to one of pure competition.

O'Neal initially delivered strong financial results, and Merrill Lynch quickly became the most profitable investment bank in the United States. This, in turn, allowed O'Neal, essentially, to choose his own board; he handpicked nine of the eleven directors, and several of these nine were close friends and former associates of his from GM. O'Neal managed to further escape oversight when Jill K. Conway resigned as the lead independent director on Merrill Lynch's board in May 2007 and was never replaced. Although a lead director is not required by law, not having one is a "major governance gap," according to Sonnenfeld.

Things fell apart quickly when the bottom dropped out of the subprime mortgage market; Merrill Lynch was forced to write down more than $8 billion, the largest loss in the history of the firm. Then it was reported that O'Neal had approached another bank, Wachovia, about bailing him out by merging with Merrill Lynch, and that he had done so without consulting his board. This cost him the support of the board—NPR called the board reaction a "corporate mutiny"—and he was asked to resign, but he left with a total compensation package of $200 million.

WRONG REASONS

What lessons can be learned from O'Neal's swift ascent and subsequent derailment? From our perspective the lessons are neither new nor surprising; in fact they are quite predictable. O'Neal's derailment can be traced to three sets of distinct factors.

First, he was hired by the Merrill Lynch board to deal with a single issue—cutting costs and tightening management practices—*with no consideration of his track record as a leader*. CCL's research on executive selection indicates that top leaders are typically brought in to address one or two burning organizational needs. In other words, long-term success is sacrificed for the sake of short-term fixes and performance touch-ups.

Second, O'Neal was hired by the board based on his technical skill as an analyst and cost cutter, as a "numbers guy"—again, *with no consideration of his track record as a leader*. This is also consistent with CCL's research on executive selection. In CCL's studies the single most commonly identified strength among newly appointed senior executives was *technical expertise*. Furthermore, whereas *specific functional background* was identified as a key candidate requirement in nearly two-thirds of executive selection decisions, *leadership skill* was identified as a candidate requirement in less than one out of three cases.

Third, there is the issue of O'Neal's personality. The reason his personality was a problem requires a bit of additional commentary. Our approach to these issues depends on three major assumptions, all well supported by research.

The first assumption is that leadership matters; beyond luck, leadership is the key to organizational success or failure. This assumption may seem obvious, but it is not necessarily shared by many business school faculties or the boards of major corporations.

The second assumption is that personality drives leadership style—that who you are determines how you lead. Some people have more talent for leadership than others, and if you are one of those people who lacks talent for leadership, then you should take steps to remedy the problem or risk failure.

The third assumption is that the fundamental tasks of leadership involve building and maintaining a high-performing team, developing a constituency that supports the efforts of the team, and guiding the team to victory.

PERSONALITY WOES

Research shows that managers typically fail for eleven reasonably well-defined personality-based reasons, all of which are associated with an inability to build a team.

Fiorina, for example, displayed an arrogance that resulted in her alienating her staff, ignoring feedback, and blaming failing corporate results on subordinates. O'Neal fell victim to a syndrome that involves toughness, insensitivity to staff morale, and a tendency to use silence as a weapon and to be a loner who avoids communication.

O'Neal has been described in the business press as private, uncommunicative, aloof, steely, unflinching, and brusque. These tendencies led to a number of specific behaviors with negative implications for leadership.

For example, Merrill Lynch insiders report that O'Neal personally fired many of his top executives and used the occasion to humiliate them, a process that created enormous anger, fear, and resentment among those who remained with the organization. In addition, O'Neal surrounded himself with like-minded people, discouraged dissent, and suppressed constructive dialogue and debate during strategy sessions.

Moreover, one important task of leadership is to manage conflict within the team; in contrast, O'Neal ignored and possibly encouraged conflict among his subordinates by pitting them against one another. The negative impact of his behavior on subordinates is reflected in the fact that they began leaving in droves well in advance of the markdown fiasco.

Finally, O'Neal preferred to keep to himself and had great disdain for *schmoozing*. In the end his relations with the board members—many of them former friends and associates—became strained.

As a result of the way O'Neal treated people, when the organization's performance and numbers plummeted, he was left with no support. It is amazing how much outrageous, rude, and abusive behavior people will tolerate from bosses as long as those bosses deliver good results. But when results turn south, tolerance goes away. More generally, however, the O'Neal saga is one more illustration of the problems that occur when people are chosen for leadership positions in the absence of evidence that they have any talent for leadership.

UNUSED RESOURCE

Interestingly, personality is a powerful predictor of one's interpersonal and leadership style. Further, personality is quite easy to reliably and accurately assess with well-developed psychological assessment tools. Personality tests are widely used, with great success, in making a range of selection decisions, from customer service employees to salespeople to police officers and, yes, even janitors.

CCL's research on selection, however, indicates that personality assessments are rarely used to hire senior executives. Evidently, decisions makers assume that people skills and interpersonal style are more important for custodial staff than for senior leadership—an assumption that most people would recognize as foolhardy.

Getting on Board: Involving Directors in Leader Development

Barbara Neisendorf and Scott Saslow

In addressing the many challenges of running a high-impact executive development program, organizations can now enlist the support of a powerful ally that has a vested interest in a strong executive cadre: the board of directors.

One of the biggest challenges for those responsible for designing and delivering executive development programs is getting sufficient buy-in from the organization's most senior leaders. If the organization's CEO is a proponent of executive development, life is good—the rest of top management typically endorses the development initiatives and is often personally and actively involved in developmental activities, and development even aligns with such other business pursuits as strategic planning and business development. Indeed, progressive organizations use executive development initiatives to advance organizational strategy and to help cascade strategy from the executive suite to frontline managers.

In many organizations, however, although some individuals may recognize the importance of executive development programs and activities, it is a constant struggle to sell and reinforce their value in order to keep them funded—and alive. Ironically, when an organization reaches a crossroads of change, leader development activities are often seen as a hindrance rather than an enabler. At a time when leaders' talents are being stretched in response to a reorganization or a major change in business strategy, development is typically granted little attention.

But today there is a relatively new influence on executive development and realization of its value to the organization—boards of directors, whose role has evolved in recent years. Boards are being thrust into closer contact with both their organizations' business operations and the people running those operations. This is a unique time, when several factors are contributing to a great opportunity for development professionals to support boards of directors in their role, which is increasingly focused on people development activities. As with supporting the CEO, aligning with and supporting the board provides instant credibility and support for senior development professionals. Boards are a largely untapped resource—not many organizations have really engaged them in executive development—but for those that have, the payoff can be huge.

IRON IS HOT

Why is this the right time to involve boards in executive development? In the past, boards' interest in people issues was typically limited to CEO succession and executive compensation, for which boards are legally responsible. However, boards' activities and the content they address are now changing, for several reasons. First and foremost is legislation enacted in 2002 that has been giving corporations compliance headaches: the Sarbanes-Oxley Act (named for its sponsors, Senator Paul Sarbanes, D-Maryland, and Representative Michael G. Oxley, R-Ohio).

Sarbanes-Oxley—sometimes known as SOX or SarbOx—has pushed boards into deeper involvement with people issues through its Title IV ("Enhanced Financial Disclosures"), which establishes a "Code of Ethics for Senior Financial Officers." Companies often expand these principles of right and wrong into a code of conduct outlining expected behavior for all employees. An important implication for human resource departments is that behaviors are clearly affected by developmental activities. As the board is responsible for helping to define this code and deliver it throughout the organization, it is faced with a monumental development challenge, both for current management and future leaders. This is where HR's products and board responsibilities coincide: what the board needs—a strong, ethical body of executive leaders—is what HR can deliver best. The question is, is HR up to it? Can HR frame executive development in a way that meets these critical board expectations?

The work of boards in the area of succession has been, classically, confined to the narrow task of CEO succession, unconnected to both management succession and executive development. Boards have simply not had a say in such matters. But that lack of involvement is nearing an end. Boards are starting to demand information and involvement in overall management succession because they now feel the heat for what goes on inside the company, including management behavior and corporate culture.

The health of the organization's leadership is a key indicator of the organization's ability to successfully execute its business plan, and boards must now vouch for that ability. This requires that the information available to boards go beyond succession lists and be reviewed more often than just once a year.

Boards may be reluctant to involve themselves more fully in executive development work for one key reason—they have typically not been good at it. In a 2004 study by global management consulting firm A. T. Kearney, all board members agreed that leadership development and succession planning are important, but only 25 percent believed that they were very proficient at these activities.

Some boards are changing their composition to address this issue. According to "The New Recruit," an article in the September 2005 issue of *Human Resource Executive*, a few boards are nominating HR executives to their ranks in order to gain these individuals' expertise and focus.

Another factor that is moving boards to take a more substantial role in executive development is CEO turnover. Executive outplacement firm Challenger, Gray & Christmas reported in 2005 that CEO turnover was running a whopping 53 percent higher than in the previous year and that the final rate for the year was likely to surpass the record set in 2000. Because of this turnover, if development of senior talent isn't monitored at a higher level—in other words, by the board—development initiatives are likely to be suspended or rebuilt every few years, resulting in loss of momentum and hence of impact on the executive group. Boards, as an element of their fiduciary responsibilities, have to ensure the quality of company management.

For evidence of another influence on board behavior, one has only to look at the number of articles on executive development that have appeared in *Harvard Business Review* and *McKinsey Quarterly*, favorite intellectual watering holes for CEOs. "The View from the Boardroom," an article in McKinsey's 2005 special issue on value and performance, reported on the key issues board members want to spend more time on; five of the top seven are related to executive development. These seven, in order, with development-related topics in italics, are *talent and skills*, strategy and risk, *developing management, evaluation of top management, evaluation of CEO performance*, current company performance, and *CEO succession*.

According to an October 2005 article in *HBR*, "Growing Talent as If Your Business Depended on It," "Many executives believe that leadership development is a job for the HR Department. This may be the single biggest misconception they can have." The implication is that although HR needs to support the development process with methods and tools, line executives and top managers also need to take executive development under their wing. The article goes on to state that "if line managers are held responsible for executing the talent development initiatives, the board should assume high-level ownership of the overall system." Such board ownership is a hallmark of highly evolved succession management processes.

These are the forces that boards are responding to in demanding more involvement in executive development and succession. Three of the top drivers are legislative pressure, turnover of CEOs and corporate officers, and a groundswell of popular opinion that holds that boards should shoulder more responsibility. So if a board expects to play a role in this arena, what can you as a leader do to partner with this newfound ally?

POWER UP

Here are five things leaders can do to leverage the power of the board in executive development:

Ensure that succession integrates with business planning. Too often succession planning and business planning are completely separate activities, the first owned by HR and the second by the CEO. Because the business plan is simply a combination of opportunities weighed against capabilities, the organization, to properly construct a strategic plan, must consider current and future talent. There can be disastrous consequences when the strategic plan and succession plan are developed separately. For one, a company may fail to recognize that it lacks the appropriate talent to execute a new strategy. Or as is more often the case, the company may waste executive development resources in ways that negatively affect a new business direction. The business press has featured a lot of rhetoric about the importance of intertwining development with core business processes, but the starting point for this integration is in the planning process itself. When a new strategy is being evaluated, the board must surface succession and development considerations at the same time.

To support the board in this, HR must make a few changes:

- Increase collaboration in succession planning, shifting it from an HR process to a business process.
- Align the milestones and approval timelines for succession with timelines in the business planning process.
- Provide tools and templates that equip leaders to perform succession work in conjunction with strategic planning.
- Take an active role, and facilitate combined discussion on strategic planning and succession.
- Ensure that succession and development issues are a part of the dialogue at each stage of strategy development, whether HR is in the room or not.

These are important foundational steps in harnessing the board's power in support of development.

Directly involve the board in succession planning. According to a board member of a $3 billion diversified manufacturing company, "The absolutely clear, nondelegable responsibility of the board is CEO succession. Very close behind is how the board today has an immense interest in CFO performance and succession. For the board not to be active in a significant way in CFO succession is a mistake. As to succession in other key management roles, a company cannot fail to look very carefully at its bench strength and know what it really would do if it loses its chief marketing officer, chief information officer, or others at that level. This has to be part of an active, continuing conversation between the board and top management, especially since retention level and bench strength are directly tied to board-level issues."

When it comes to succession, boards increasingly want to be able to vouch for the whole body of leadership, not just the CEO. Boards now assert their need to know about bench strength for all key positions. This means they expect to receive more information on the successors for a number of management posts—as many as thirty of the top positions.

HR must help the board do several things:

- Understand which key positions drive corporate performance.
- Assess incumbents, successors, external talent, and longer-term high-potentials.
- Keep an eye on the development plans, and discuss progress in board agendas.
- Engage in frequent discussions about bench strength and retention.

This moves board succession discussions from perfunctory annual presentations to an ongoing, dynamic dialogue on talent. Just receiving prepared information isn't enough, though. The next step requires even more board involvement.

Help the board get to know and grow the talent. A board member of a $2 billion manufacturing company says: "When companies have a sales meeting, a reward weekend, or other high-level events, it is a grand opportunity for board directors to take time to get at the fiber of the people in important positions and be prepared to talk to and about those people. Or when there's a board retreat, it is mighty important for directors to be around senior management other than who they are around all the time."

Directors have a fiduciary responsibility to know the organization's executives and how they will behave when no one is looking. So boards are looking for more opportunities to get acquainted with the people entrusted with operational decision making. They need the benefit of formal and informal information on the ethical soundness of these critical leaders, and some of this information needs to be provided independent of the CEO. To this end HR should encourage independent interaction between the board and individual leaders, although not always staging these interactions.

HR can pave the way for board members to do the following:

- Sponsor high-level project teams.
- Directly coach succession candidates.
- Visit candidates' operating units in different parts of the world.
- Observe presentations by leaders outside of board meetings.
- Participate in company leadership development courses.
- Implement a committee dedicated to human capital, one that goes beyond the scope of the compensation committee.
- Participate in the planning and implementation of development.
- Informally assess leaders at social events and recreational outings.

In the process, directors will gain a personal sense of individual leaders and the overall cadre of top talent. That knowledge is indispensable to directors' accountability for guaranteeing ethical leadership for the organization.

Enable the board to evaluate leaders' performance and ethical behavior. According to the CEO of a $145 million high-tech firm: "Having a leader in a key position who is not aligned with corporate values and culture can be enormously detrimental, to the point that it can unravel the company's performance. Alignment with corporate values doesn't necessarily guarantee you're going to be successful, but if you're not aligned, you won't be successful in the long run."

One responsibility that has emerged for board members is to know and vouch for the character of the company's leaders—a checks-and-balances role. Boards that can unreservedly stand behind the character of the organization's leaders are better positioned to protect the long-term interests of the company. But the reality is that there has been intense pressure from Wall Street over the past fifteen to twenty years to focus on short-term results. Corporate executives have felt this pressure to deliver outstanding results every quarter and have sometimes let the pressure prevail over sound management. But with the ensuing negative and sometimes disastrous consequences, boards are now setting a clear mandate that companies reward results that are achieved in accordance with corporate values and that support long-term aims.

HR can do several things to support the board in this area:

- Ensure that the executive compensation system rewards profits with principles, weighing issues of conduct fairly along with business results.
- Discuss character and alignment with corporate values and culture as part of succession planning.
- Strengthen the interviewing process for officer positions by taking a good, hard look at all candidates, both internal and external; presenting candidates with business-based ethical dilemmas and scenarios that have no clear right or wrong answer to see how they respond; and

conducting extensive reference checks that probe ethical and responsible decision making.

- Hold management responsible for employee and customer satisfaction, and conduct surveys to get an unfiltered view of these perceptions.

Present and future leaders should be assessed and developed around an ethical core focused on character and values-based decision making. Ultimately, this is how a board and CEO can foster trust that there will be ethical and responsible leadership now and in the future.

Focus on the tone at the top. A board member of a $3 billion diversified operations organization says: "The best managed and most admired companies always find something that tracks a shared sense of values and mission—not an off-the-shelf statement of core values but something that is drawn from the culture of the organization that people can relate to and regard as part of their job to enforce. The board can and should help develop and nurture this."

Have the board and CEO identified the values that constitute the bedrock of the company? Has management examined how these values apply to business situations involving sales, customer relations, and employee relations? The tone at the top—the behavior of leaders—is a bellwether for long-term corporate success. This fact is referred to again and again by those who have investigated recent cases of corporate wrongdoing. Boards have a responsibility to oversee a culture of shared values and behaviors. It is up to the board to ensure that management has implemented a code of conduct that is values based and to hold management accountable for living these values.

HR, management, and the board can work together to do the following:

- Define the company's DNA of integrity: the corporate values that underpin the company's success and the way things get done.

- Continuously engage employees and managers in discussions about what constitutes ethical behavior.
- Make values and ethical behavior permanent components of all developmental activities.
- Establish and enforce consequences for code-of-conduct violations by acting clearly, swiftly, and consistently and bringing all cases in front of the board.

The board's focus should be on developing leaders who are personally committed, credible, and willing to take action on the values they espouse. It is incumbent on the board to ensure that these values are authentic and that they set the tone for the behavior of people throughout the organization.

NEW ALLY

In the midst of business as usual, people in HR can find an unexpected ally in the organization's corporate directors. Although developing top talent has been an important organizational issue for years, it has taken on a new importance in the eyes of the board. Organizations would do well to catch this rising tide, albeit with care. The board must be involved on its own terms, in the context of its priorities: long-term, sustainable business success and an appreciation for the concerns of all stakeholders. For HR this means that executive development must be inexorably linked to the business strategy and must stay ahead of any changes to the business plan. Succession must be much more than just the annual preparation of encyclopedic binders. More important, ethical behavior and the tone that it sets must be elevated to a top consideration.

Executive development has come a long way in just the past decade, and involving boards of directors more closely is another stage in the continued progress of such development. For executive development to drive lasting, organization-wide value, boards must play a significant role.

Generations Talk About Leaders and Leadership Development

Alessia D'Amato and Kelly M. Hannum

The challenges of the global financial crisis may have changed the number of people looking for a job, but they haven't changed the need to attract, retain, and develop the best talent. In fact, as many organizations are being reduced to working with skeleton crews, the need to attract and maintain a high-potential workforce may be increasing and the tools with which to do so may be decreasing. A key ingredient of retaining and developing a talented workforce is understanding the expectations of managers.

CCL analyzed data from a survey of 1,538 individuals in various managerial roles in fifty-two organizations in Europe. These data provided insights into managers' needs and wishes for development across generations. These managers worked in international corporations and were spread across managerial levels—15 percent were senior executives, 29 percent were in upper management, and the rest were in middle management or lower, 33 percent and 23 percent, respectively. The generational groups were early baby boomers (born between 1946 and 1951, 6 percent), late boomers (born between 1952 and 1959, 23 percent), early Generation Xers (born between 1960 and 1970, 45 percent), and late Gen Xers (born between 1971 and 1980, 26 percent).

The initial question that the survey sought to answer was, "Do older and younger people want different things in their leaders?" Managers were asked to identify and rank the top five attributes that they want in their leaders. People across the generations agreed on one such attribute: each group wanted leaders to be credible and farsighted. Managers in the early boomers group wanted their leaders to delegate more often. One potential reason for this is that older managers have accumulated significant experience and now want more control and autonomy. Managers in the late Gen Xers group indicated that they wanted to be trusted by their leaders. Managers in this group have often reached their positions faster than earlier generations did, and now are striving for status and recognition.

A leader who is a good coach is desired across all generational groups but is most important to younger managers. This desire of younger managers for leaders who coach or mentor them may reflect the changing nature of the workplace. In years past, development was a job for the human resource department; nowadays people in leadership positions need to be prepared to meet this challenge. Managers are increasingly assessed on how well they have developed their subordinates. The good news is that when younger leaders are nurtured they will pass their knowledge and expertise on to the next generation in the workforce.

Preparing the present workforce is also preparing the way for the future. Research indicates that being a mentor has benefits for both the mentor and the mentee. In fact, managers can become more effective and efficient in their jobs when they mentor others. For example, they can gain information and support and expand their power base and reputation. They may be seen by their bosses and upper management as having good judgment, reputation, and credibility, which may result in their advancement, increased recognition, influence, clout, visibility, legitimacy, respect, and admiration.

As a manager, what actions can you take to improve your mentoring?

- Concentrate on acting as a mentor to your direct reports.
- Promote your direct reports and trumpet their praises.
- Coach your direct reports on how to meet expectations.
- Provide prompt feedback, both positive and constructive.

- Help your followers learn from their mistakes.
- Provide challenges and opportunities to your followers.
- Set a challenging climate, and encourage the development of your followers.

In short, the more you mentor your followers, the better you will be as a performer.

The second question examined was, "What are the expectations of each generation about the nature of development opportunities?" Individuals from each generational group indicated that learning and development were important for their careers. All generations indicated a preference for developing skills in team building, problem solving, decision making, and strategic planning.

Building an effective team requires leadership that creates an overarching framework—coordinating individual contributions and collective effort. Managers' ability to recruit and manage talented individuals is the foundation for creating a high-performance team. However, managers must also focus on developing relationships among team members that foster the sharing of diverse experiences—functional expertise as well as ideas and perspectives. Various strategies can be engaged for development in team building. Shadowing a successful team leader might be the best developmental assignment for emerging leaders, but managers from older generations might find it more effective to work with a successful team leader in establishing a new project team.

Developing problem-solving and decision-making abilities has typically involved improving the skills of clarifying problems, analyzing causes, detecting options, and implementing the best solutions. An alternative perspective suggests envisioning the problem as well as desired outcomes jointly with the main stakeholders before seeking a solution. Managers can focus on understanding the current and ideal states from different perspectives in order to work toward an optimum solution. For any generation, valuable developmental assignments might focus on reviewing recent decisions and analyzing the processes by which decisions were made.

This review might be performed with an executive coach in a one-on-one setting or in a peer-mentoring session. Another approach might be to spend time in a variety of functional units in order to better understand different processes and perspectives.

Strategic planning is a process for determining where an organization is going in the medium to long term—typically a three- to five-year time frame. Leadership practices for defining and implementing business strategy need to be groomed and enhanced through experiential activities. For instance, having new managers sit in on strategy discussions can develop their understanding of the process. In addition, having strategy discussions with managers at lower organizational levels not only informs an organization's strategy but also builds those managers' skills in strategic thinking and planning and illuminates the connections between day-to-day managerial tasks and longer-term organizational goals.

A developmental area indicated as important by all generations except the youngest one is managing change. Effective change-management skills include improving resource efficiency and performance, communicating activities and events, and understanding the types and levels of support needed by different groups and individuals. A good understanding of managing change helps managers think creatively about the business operation and overall performance improvement—not just in terms of financial results but with a long-term perspective and strategy.

The survey results indicate that there is broad agreement on areas that all managers are interested in developing—regardless of generation—and that deeper attention than currently offered is desired for leadership development across generational groups. As a leader you can promote development in your organization by mentoring others and by focusing on the areas deemed most important across all generations—team building, problem solving, decision making, and strategic planning. Becoming a mentor benefits the mentor as well as the mentee, and in a tight economy everyone is looking for ways to reap more benefits from less effort.

Developing and Retaining Emerging Leaders

David Baldwin and Stephanie Trovas

The future effectiveness and success of your organization depends to a large degree on its rising managers and professionals under thirty-five. Training and nurturing these leaders and keeping them on board is critical—but to do so you must first understand who they are, how they think, and what they want.

In an increasingly competitive, global, and technology-driven marketplace, leaders must keep a constant vigil over the management ranks in their organizations. The ability to recruit, train, develop, and retain people for top leadership positions is essential if organizations are to succeed—or even survive—in such an environment. A big part of this challenge involves people who are members of the group sometimes known as the Millennial Generation, defined here as people born between 1984 and 2001—among them rising managers and professionals who are under thirty-five years old, that is, emerging leaders.

Some Millennials have already emerged as leaders. Some have moved into middle management and some have even risen to vice president or C-level executive positions and are already in crucial positions and playing a major role in deciding strategic direction. A number of Millennials have started high-tech companies. In fact, according to the *Los Angeles Times*, approximately 70 percent of current start-up businesses in the United States were founded by people under thirty-six. And in some companies, Millennials are being promoted above older colleagues.

The focus of this article, however, is on people who are just beginning to take on significant leadership and management roles. Researchers, management experts, and leaders of organizations have all been devoting a lot of effort to understanding how to prepare these emerging leaders, how to work most effectively with them, and how to make the best use of their distinctive skills and talents. Three considerations are important when trying to gain insight into emerging leaders:

- There are fewer managers to choose from and develop in this age group than there were in preceding generations.
- Evolving employment patterns have affected this generation's attitudes toward employers.
- The newest generation of managers views authority differently than previous generations did, and this has a notable impact on emerging leaders' attitudes toward leadership.

A SMALLER POOL

One of the unique challenges of working with emerging leaders is demographic. To put it simply, there are too few of them. Although the Millennial Generation has almost as many members (seventy-five million) as the baby boom generation (the seventy-six million people born between 1946 and 1963), most of them are too young to have risen to emerging-leader status. And Generation

X (those born between 1964 and 1983) has only sixty-six million members to fill the leadership ranks. In the past, organizations usually had a sizable pool of adequately trained people to draw on for managerial and leadership positions, but now the number of workers with the skills needed to take on the critical leadership challenges companies face is smaller. The meteoric rise of the technology industry during the 1990s is another factor. That industry has created new places for younger workers, spreading the workers who are qualified or have potential for leadership positions across old-economy and new-economy companies and so reducing the number available to either.

The consequence is that established leaders must take even more care to make sure that emerging leaders are developed—even though changing work patterns and worker attitudes make this task more challenging than in the past.

CHANGING THE CONTRACT

Since the 1970s, employment patterns have been undergoing fundamental changes. For instance, the implicit understanding that employers and employees have about their relationship—sometimes referred to as the *psychological work contract*—has changed. Employees no longer expect to stay with one company for their entire career; in fact, emerging leaders have little expectation of remaining with the same company for even ten years. Estimates of the number of organizations that emerging leaders will work for by the time they reach age sixty-five vary from six to ten. Hanging onto emerging leaders for the long term has thus become a serious concern for many organizations.

This change in the psychological work contract has been cited by some people who look askance at Millennials and, before them, Gen Xers. However, this change has come about not just because of Millennials and Gen Xers but because of other generations as well. So even though it has been suggested that Millennials and Gen Xers are not willing to pay their dues as previous generations did, the reality is that many emerging leaders, a good number of whom saw their parents suffer through downsizings, simply don't trust an organization to be there for them in the long term. And emerging leaders tend to believe that people should be promoted, compensated, and given responsibility based on how competent they are rather than on how long they have been in the workforce or with a single company.

Another change in employment patterns has been a shift away from the traditional hierarchy. In the past it was generally accepted that younger people would report to older people, but now it is becoming more common for younger people to be promoted over their elders. In some industries and competitive environments—the Internet marketplace, for example—the general perception is that younger employees have some skills and abilities that older workers don't. This not only creates generational conflict but also raises the possibility that some emerging leaders are being thrust into positions before they have had the opportunity to develop the necessary management and leadership skills.

EARNED ESTEEM

Past generations tended to at least acknowledge if not always acquiesce to positional authority, but many if not most emerging leaders do not accord people respect just for their rank. Emerging leaders frequently don't acknowledge authority or assume that it arises from position. Their prevailing view of authority can be summed up as, "Don't listen to leaders until they prove they can actually do the work themselves." If managers can't demonstrate that they can accomplish work themselves in addition to getting others to do it, emerging leaders are unlikely to grant them the same degree of authority as previous generations did. Emerging leaders expect managers to earn their stripes and don't give much weight to superior position or long experience.

That attitude about authority is frequently taken as an indication of disrespect for elders in general and bosses in

particular. However, emerging leaders' viewpoint may be more aptly described as skepticism—bosses need to prove that they are still capable. This skepticism may arise from the fact that emerging leaders came of age with few heroes or leaders they could claim as their own—scandals, for example, removed a number of potential political heroes. It may also be a result of emerging leaders having been raised in a period of heightened consumer marketing, which may have succeeded primarily in making them suspicious of anything that smacks of hype—perhaps including overblown war stories about being "self-made" told by leaders of the organizations in which they work.

This skeptical view may also be rooted in the limited experience that emerging leaders have in the workplace. In their organizations, managers from a previous generation may have proved their technical expertise years before the emerging leaders came on board. As the older workers shifted from technical to managerial positions, they developed leadership skills that complemented but were different from the technical skills that carried them through the earlier stages of their careers. Newer workers don't see those technical skills and may assume they don't exist, which reinforces their doubts about managerial authority. Alternatively, technological changes may have, at least in the view of emerging leaders, outpaced the older managers' technical skills.

WHAT THEY WANT

Examining emerging leaders' core values and preferences about leadership reveals how they may prefer to behave as leaders and how they want their bosses to act. Emerging leaders prefer a hands-off approach in leading others and in being led, with an emphasis on delegation. Additionally, they prefer honest and direct communication and feedback, an openness to changing directions quickly, pragmatism, a career path or development plan, and a relaxed, casual work environment.

Emerging leaders do respect authenticity and the ability to get things done, so a good approach when working with them—an approach that will lend itself to achieving good results—is to focus on tactics that communicate authenticity and sincerity. Managers of emerging leaders may also find it effective to act as mentors and develop personal relationships with them to understand what motivates them as individuals. Although more research needs to be done, it appears that this relationship approach to developing emerging leaders may be critical to helping them.

Emerging leaders' attitudes toward leadership and authority are influenced by the times in which they came of age. The members of each generation are to some degree similarly affected by important events that occur during critical times in their lives and development. To understand today's emerging leaders, it is useful to take note of the important events that occurred as they grew up.

These events seem to have influenced emerging leaders to behave in ways consistent with self-protection. The consequences of corporate downsizings and government scandals appear to be significant drivers of their behavior. Moreover, emerging leaders tend to want to establish themselves in their careers and to build their résumés before committing to having a family. One piece of evidence is that this generation is marrying later than previous generations. According to *The New York Times Almanac* for 2001, in 1998, the median age at which men first married was twenty-seven, and for women, twenty-five. In 1960, men married at a median age of twenty-three and women at a median age of twenty.

It's also useful to consider the social trends during the years in which Millennials grew up. Divorce rates skyrocketed, and children's quality time with their parents diminished. Millennials were immersed in technology, which advanced by leaps and bounds and whose influence burgeoned.

All of these factors influenced perceptions, values, and beliefs about the world in general and leadership specifically. They predisposed emerging leaders to have less certainty, trust, and loyalty than previous generations did.

To understand emerging leaders—and to develop and retain them—it's also helpful to know their defining characteristics and what they expect from the workplace. Research by CCL and others has identified some of these characteristics and expectations, and although they can exist for individuals from any generation, they are more pronounced in emerging leaders.

Characteristics. Emerging leaders tend to be technologically savvy, independent, and skeptical of institutions and hierarchy. They are entrepreneurial risk takers who think globally, learn experientially, and embrace change. They are efficient and focused on outcomes, open to and appreciative of differences, and socially responsible.

Workplace expectations. Emerging leaders tend to prefer direct communication and informality. They value freedom, flexibility, and a sense of community. Work-life balance is important to them—quality of life takes precedence over money. They want continuous and immediate feedback, an individually customized development plan, and a genuine relationship with a mentor or coach. They want their work to be meaningful and challenging, and they expect their rewards to be immediate.

FREE AGENTS

Some if not most emerging leaders have agendas to build their skills and résumés, with the aim of giving themselves a sense of job security beyond their current organizations. They appear to be more committed to the vocation than to the organization. The free-agency concept popularized in professional sports is an apt metaphor for the attitude emerging leaders carry into the workplace: they will stay with an organization as long as it's the best offer on the table. Savvy companies that are aware of this agenda, such as Intel and Nike, are providing opportunities for their emerging leaders to leave the organization, acquire skills elsewhere, then be rehired in a new capacity.

Why should organizations invest in the development of emerging leaders who are liable to job hop to the next opportunity available?

First, organizations need to accept that they will not be able to keep all of their emerging leaders. Second, organizations that are aware of the needs of emerging leaders and are willing to take the time to build a trusting relationship, which includes providing challenging opportunities for growth, may well be able to reap the benefits of extended employment and commitment. For example, at Bank of America, newly hired emerging leaders are offered a one-year investment program similar to an extended graduate school program. They are provided a mentor, they work on projects involving real-world problems and present their solutions to upper management, and they receive feedback on their work from their peers and their boss. The program is aimed at fostering the emerging leaders' trust in the company by making them feel they are part of a community of peers and the organization is investing in their future. The long-term success of this development and retention strategy remains to be confirmed by experience. But one thing is certain: when investment and challenge end, emerging leaders begin to look elsewhere.

Understanding how emerging leaders view trust in an organizational system can be complicated. Some emerging leaders have suggested that they give and receive trust in exchange for the freedom to accomplish work on their terms. As one emerging leader said:

> *More freedom gets people to do things. Organizations must be grounded in choice. I want to feel empowered. I want my organization to assume that people do want to work hard. I don't want to be micromanaged. They need to realize that if they give you freedom, they'll keep you. Tapping into the people—empowering and motivating versus power, authority, control, and position [is what is important].*

Although emerging leaders want independence in accomplishing their work, they appear to also want a sense of community, of belonging to a group of people who are as committed as they are. At times the need for independence and the need for community can collide and result in personal tension for emerging leaders, and this is a phenomenon that merits further attention in devising effective leadership development for emerging leaders.

Emerging leaders want authentic relationships with their mentors and other coworkers. They want to be appreciated for what they do rather than be told they are too young or don't have enough experience. Consider these two comments:

> *I want to be mentored by and to mentor the older generation, too. We learn together. I would like the older generation to be open to being taught. I can learn from them; I want to know why they think they don't have anything to learn from us.*

> *I need an organization that is patient and understanding as I ask lots of questions. I feel inexperienced and know that I'll make some mistakes. It helps if people are open to listening and sharing experiences.*

Emerging leaders also have a thirst for feedback—both receiving it and giving it. They want to know when they are doing well and when they're not—and they prefer to know immediately rather than through a yearly performance review.

The current economic climate and vying for top talent have made retention an increasingly critical human resource issue. Organizations can adopt a number of tactics to retain under-35 employees in general and emerging leaders in particular. Most of these tactics involve nonmonetary reward systems such as vacation time, employee control over schedules, developmental opportunities, positive reinforcement and acknowledgment from people whom younger workers respect, coaching, and mentoring. As one emerging leader put it:

Organizations need to know how to reward without using money; money isn't the reward desired. We need to keep variety in our jobs. We need help in figuring out where we're going. We want job-pathing and development. We want expectations that we can understand.

TAKING ACTION

It's not overstating things to say that the current and future effectiveness and success of organizations is in the hands of emerging leaders. Established leaders can take a number of specific steps to develop and retain emerging leaders:

- Listen to and follow their input on how they would like to be developed.
- Offer them control over their time and space.
- Provide short-term, performance-based rewards.
- Be available as a mentor.
- Provide the resources they need.
- Give timely and consistent feedback.
- Encourage a fun, relaxed environment.
- Offer choices of on-the-job training.
- Assess their motivation, and find out what kind of perks and benefits they want.
- Introduce entrepreneurial opportunities.
- Give them ownership of their work and responsibility for bottom-line results.

Next Generation: What Leaders Need to Know About Millennials

Kris Downing

It's a unique time in the workplace as four generations of workers are intermingling. As the most recent generation enters the workforce, the challenge for leaders is not only to understand the differences between the generations but also to embrace their different perspectives and find ways to bring out the best in everyone.

Generational differences are alive and well in the U.S. workplace, and understanding these differences will help us prepare for future leadership challenges. For perhaps the first time ever, we are seeing four generations of workers at once. According to a 2004 report from the U.S. Bureau of Labor Statistics, twenty-three million workers aged fifty-five and over shared workspace with twenty-two million workers aged sixteen to twenty-four, thirty-two million aged twenty-five to thirty-four, and sixty-nine million aged thirty-five to fifty-four. The relative proportions among these groups are projected to remain about the same through 2014, except for workers fifty-five and over (whose numbers are expected to grow about 4 percent as people retire later in life). Each of these demographic groups is unique and has distinct characteristics, which raises the question, *How can they work together?*

A survey conducted in 2001 by Bridge Works, a company that explores generational issues in the workplace and the marketplace, turned up some interesting statistics:

- One-third of respondents said they were often offended at work by someone from another generation.

- About a quarter of Traditionalists (here defined as being born before 1946), 30 percent of baby boomers (born between 1946 and 1963), and more than 60 percent of Generation Xers (born between 1964 and 1983) said their generation is not viewed positively by the other generations.
- Seventy percent of Traditionalists said that a lifetime career with one company is a good goal; only 35 percent of boomers and 17 percent of Gen Xers agreed.

DEFINING EVENTS

The newest generation of workers, those born between 1984 and 2001, wasn't included in the survey. This fourth generation entering the workforce has been called Generation Y (because it follows Generation X) or, as a play on words, Generation Why?—a reference to its members' apparent strong desire for choice and comfort. Generation Y is also sometimes called the Net Generation (referring to the exponentially greater role of the Internet and technology in the lives of these new workers). Increasingly, however, Millennial Generation is the name most commonly used to describe those born between 1984 and 2001.

Every generation has defining world events. For Traditionalists, the major one was World War II. Early baby boomers have strong memories of the assassinations of John F. Kennedy, Robert F. Kennedy, and Martin Luther King Jr. For later baby boomers it was the Watergate scandal and the resignation of President Richard M. Nixon. For Generation X, memorable events include the Challenger space shuttle explosion, the proliferation of AIDS, and the fall of the Berlin Wall. The Millennial Generation has its own key defining moments and developments:

- The terrorist attacks of September 11, 2001, and the subsequent war on terror
- The Persian Gulf and Afghanistan wars

- Widespread use of technology, especially the Internet but also sophisticated graphics in computer games and other media, cellular phones, MP3s and iPods, and digital cameras
- Natural disasters, including the Asian tsunami and Hurricane Katrina

World events provide one window into a deeper understanding of the human environment. At the same time it is important to look at particular characteristics of a generational group:

- According to global marketing research firm GfK NOP, in February 2002, 13 percent of twelve- to fourteen-year-olds in the United States had a cell phone. By December 2004, that number had jumped to 40 percent.
- CNET News.com reports that more than 50 percent of the twelve million teenagers who go online create original material for the World Wide Web—writing blogs or creating artwork, videos, and photos for personal home pages or school Web sites.
- Many Millennials have what the *Wall Street Journal* has called "helicopter parents," who remain highly involved—many would say overinvolved—in the lives of their children, even into young adulthood. A Middlebury College study found that college freshmen are in contact with their parents more than ten times a week.
- Antidepressants and other behavior-modification drugs, such as Ritalin, have been widely used by Millennials, who are identified by the Web encyclopedia Wikipedia as "one of the most medicated generations in human history."
- Today's college students use the Internet in many facets of their life, including their personal journals. Almost 20 percent of the traffic generated at LiveJournal.com originates from college-based personal computers.

PARENTAL INFLUENCE

One way to view the Millennials' distinctiveness is through the lens of their baby boomer parents. Consider this description of boomers, again from Wikipedia: "Leaders of this generation tend to reevaluate their lives in midlife, and many focus desperately on the successes and failures of their children. Increasingly, the tendency to 'micromanage' the lives of their children is expressed in this generation to a significant degree. . . . boomers seek to improve society through children."

Once grounded in this unique parent-child dimension, other descriptors of Millennials take on added meaning. Lee Rainie, director of the Pew Internet & American Life Project, gave a compelling sketch of Millennials in a recent speech to the annual conference of the Public Library Association. According to Pew Foundation research:

- Millennials are "special" and in large part have grown up well protected by their parents, who have reinforced the notion that their offspring are the key to the future, "vital to the nation and to their parents' sense of purpose." After all, remember that this generation grew up with arranged play dates, Net Nanny, television and computer parental controls, increased parental involvement in school events, mandated safety requirements such as car seats for children under age eight, and No Child Left Behind legislation. Some people even put their yet-to-be-born children on the waiting lists of elite kindergartens and hire consultants to help build their high school students' résumés.
- Millennials are confident, high achieving, and under a lot of pressure. Parents, educators, and other leaders have put tremendous emphasis on increasing self-esteem in children, setting high learning standards, and holding schools accountable for achieving these standards. This means that our newest workers are achievement oriented yet accustomed to heavy parental involvement.

- Millennials, more than any other generation, understand the power of technology as communication. "They are digital natives in a land of digital immigrants."

READY TO GO

Employers will need to continue finding ways to attract, motivate, and retain all of their bright, engaged workers, regardless of generation. However, these newest entrants into the job market pose unique challenges.

Positioning your company as a hierarchical, traditional organization won't net it a large pool of Millennial talent. Because of the confident nature of Millennials, they are looking to contribute immediately to an organization and are not willing to wait years before being heard. In a recent article in *Fast Company*, a twenty-two-year-old marketing associate with a major corporation echoed these sentiments by saying, "That's what we want from employers—a chance to learn, to be challenged, to be taken seriously."

Another element to consider is that in recruiting Millennials you also need to make a positive impression on their involved parents. Facing the reality of helicopter parents, a number of large companies are finding ways to involve these parents in the recruiting process, such as sending them welcome packets or including them in initial informational sessions. A recent *Wall Street Journal* article stated that "candidates are stalling on job offers to consult with their parents. Parents are calling hiring managers to protest pay packages and trying to renegotiate."

Clearly, the effective use of technology is critical for Millennials. Consider, for example, the recent increase in the use of *smart mob* technology, which enables people to connect instantaneously to information and other people, allowing a form of social coordination. Here's how Howard Rheingold, who coined the term in his book *Smart Mobs: The Next Social Revolution* (Perseus, 2002), describes the concept: "Smart mobs emerge when communication and computing technologies amplify human talents for cooperation. The impacts of smart mob technology already appear to be both beneficial and destructive, used by some of its earliest adopters to support democracy and by others to coordinate terrorist attacks. A million Filipinos toppled President Estrada through public demonstrations organized through salvos of text messages."

It is worthwhile to note Lee Rainie's assessment of the Millennials' technology of choice for communication. That choice is less about having a preference for a particular technological device and more about convenience and situation in that "their information and communication needs are contextual and contingent. They like to get material they want on a cell phone when that's the gizmo in their hand. Similarly, they like [instant messaging] when they are sitting at a computer. They like browsing Web sites when they are on a general search, and yes, we hear they like books and magazines when they are settling down to immerse themselves in a subject."

SOCIAL NETWORKS

Training and education designed for Millennials need to be multisensory, rapid fire, on demand, and compelling. According to a recent article in *Fast Company*, Michelle Lapierre, senior director of customer relationship marketing at Marriott International, is "developing bite-size 'edutainment' training podcasts so workers can download information to their cell phones, laptops, and iPods as they need it."

Millennials also tend to be self-directed learners. When stumped by a challenge or problem, they will open up the issue to their social network and ask for advice. Millennials are also known for their ability to find answers on the Web for just about anything—instantly.

Closer examination of the Millennial Generation offers some other interesting leadership implications. In terms of *setting direction*, leaders need to connect with these newest workforce entrants in more ways than just showing them a job description.

In other words, how does an employee's daily work tie into the goals of the organization—and ultimately to goals bigger than the corporation itself? *Creating alignment* encompasses the ability to find common ground as well as find ways to work cross-culturally and cross-functionally. *Gaining commitment* from Millennials includes recognizing and responding to different motivators, whether it's work-life balance or the chance to make a difference in the company quickly.

Setting Direction

Studies indicate that Millennials have a strong need to connect their work to a higher purpose, one often greater than the company's goals. Millennials are eco-friendly—this is the generation that while growing up always participated in Earth Day. They have a high tolerance for cultural diversity; in fact they represent the most culturally diverse generation yet. Global connections are made with peers across the world. Leaders should recognize the emphasis Millennials place on contributing to the greater good and should seek to link their day-to-day work with a higher cause.

Creating Alignment

The Millennial Generation is both feedback oriented and team oriented. Millennials have played team sports, worn school uniforms, and participated in team projects at school. They quickly access their peers for opinions when faced with a problem. Rainie describes these new workers as being "more tied to group outreach and group knowledge [and] more open to cross-discipline insights." Successful leaders are comfortable in team environments and are able to encourage and inspire team performance.

Gaining Commitment

In a recent *People at Work Survey*, Mercer Human Resource Consulting discovered interesting differences between Millennials and other workers regarding commitment. "Compared to older workers, employees age eighteen to twenty-four indicate that their commitment and motivation at work are influenced less by base pay and more by promotion opportunities and flexible working arrangements. For example, 82 percent cite flexible working arrangements as a factor that influences their commitment and motivation, compared to 58 percent and 69 percent for the other employee age groups." Leaders need to understand that different motivators are at work in terms of a Millennial's commitment to work.

Millennial workers build on the desire of their older siblings (Gen Xers) for work-life balance, an issue that has been studied for almost thirty years. Research first conducted in the mid-1980s by CCL identified fifteen behavioral competencies that were empirically connected with effectiveness in leadership roles. These fifteen competencies, along with a sixteenth added later, became the core of CCL's Benchmarks® 360-degree feedback instrument. The sixteenth competency, "balance between work and personal life," was added as a value statement. In interview projects, CCL has consistently heard laments from executives who felt they had made a mistake by sacrificing time with spouses and children and for personal interests for the sake of their work. If they had it to do over again, these executives said, they would strive for a more balanced life.

As the use of Benchmarks spread and CCL's database grew, validity studies were conducted to make sure that Benchmarks was still providing an empirical link to leadership effectiveness. The good news was that the original fifteen competency scales held up well. However, the balance scale did not. In fact, there was a slightly *negative* correlation between higher balance scores and perceived effectiveness in leadership roles. It is encouraging to note, however, that when CCL replicated the research for the third time in 1999, the correlation was no longer negative but had edged up into a neutral range. So, although baby boomer managers first identified balance as being important and Gen Xers continued to raise the balance flag, it is actually Millennials who indicate that they will be true to their principles regarding work-life balance.

Consider these developments:

- Forty-eight percent of Millennials recently surveyed by consumer research and advisory firm Iconoculture indicated that they didn't have a strong desire to move up the company ladder. In fact, 80 percent wanted to work fewer hours.
- National law firm Womble Carlyle Sandridge & Rice recently implemented a part-time track so that recent law-school graduates can personalize their work schedules.
- Accounting and consulting firm Deloitte & Touche has adjusted its auditing process, which previously required associates to be on site with clients, sometimes for months at a time. New employees balked at this approach, which kept them away from their homes and families for long stretches of time. Using technology, much of the auditing work is now done remotely.

DIFFERENT STROKES

The work environment is clearly changing as we make room for four generations of employees, all of whom have different approaches to work. The leader's challenge will be not only to understand these differences but also to embrace the different perspectives and find ways to bring out the best in everyone.

The Missing Link: Organizational Culture and Leadership Development

Vidula Bal and Laura Quinn

The role that organizational culture plays in the development of leaders is crucial but often overlooked. One reason for this is that managers in charge of leadership development efforts are so embedded in their own cultures that those cultures are practically invisible to them. But there are ways to get a better picture of your own culture and determine how it might be supporting or hindering the development of leaders.

Nearly everyone has had the experience of feeling like an outsider in a different culture. When people find themselves in a place where what they see and hear is unfamiliar, they often feel awkward and nervous. And if their new surroundings are completely different from what they're used to, they might think they've landed on another planet.

Imagine that you're a sales manager making your first visit to the offices of a new client in the high-technology industry. You're excited about the visit because you have heard positive things about the company's creativity and innovation. As soon as you walk in the door, however, you start to feel uncomfortable. You're wearing a business suit, but the employees at the high-tech company are dressed casually, to put it mildly—some are wearing shorts and sandals. You fidget as you wait in the reception area. When someone comes to take you to the meeting with the company's executives, you notice as you walk through the corridors that some employees have brought their pets to work. There are a few dogs, some cats—even a ferret. When you reach the meeting room, you're astounded to see a tent set up nearby. You ask what the tent is for. "It's there for anyone who wants to take a nap," an employee explains nonchalantly.

If you had stepped into an office where the employees wore suits and where the atmosphere was closer to a traditional business environment, you probably wouldn't have given it a second thought. But you have encountered an organizational culture that is new and different to you. And although that culture is consistent with the high-tech company's focus on and support of creativity and innovation, it feels strange to you. This points up a common dualism in perceptions of organizational cultures: although people are quick to recognize cultures that are different from their own, they are usually so ensconced in their own cultures that they take them for granted and have a hard time even acknowledging their existence.

SHAPING THE CULTURE

Organizational culture is an organization's values, beliefs, practices, rites, rituals, and stories—all of which combine to make an organization unique. These cultural features often derive from the strategic business drivers of the organization—elements such as quality, innovation, results, speed, and agility. These business drivers affect policies and procedures throughout the organization, thus creating its culture.

In the example of the high-tech company, its business drivers have created an organizational culture that emphasizes casualness and physical comfort as a way to encourage and support creativity and innovation. Although you might feel as though you've stepped into a *Twilight Zone* episode, your experience during your visit is really not so unusual. You've just been turned upside-down because the company's culture has been shaped by business drivers that are different from those of your organization.

Practicing managers and academics alike have long recognized the existence of organizational cultures. Most managers, however, do not take culture into account as they devise plans and strategies for developing leaders in their organizations. One reason for this neglect is the difficulty that most people have in recognizing their own organizational cultures. But failing to acknowledge the crucial role that organizational culture plays in developing leaders can be costly. Although the culture that results from the policies and procedures affected by a company's business drivers typically reinforces those drivers, sometimes this culture ultimately works against the drivers, the company's interests, and its development goals.

CCL has focused directly on how organizations can best provide *systemic* support for leadership development. It found that many executives make the mistake of believing that merely sending employees through leadership development programs will automatically produce the quantity and types of leaders needed to handle the challenges ahead. But there is more to it than that:

to build sustainable leadership capacity, organizations must pay attention not only to development but also to the *context* in which development takes place. Organizational culture is a major part of this context, so managing the *fit* between an organization's culture and its leadership development efforts is vital to building sustainable leadership capacity.

A good way to begin your organization's leadership development efforts is to review the organization's business drivers and assess its culture. Then you can determine which kinds of developmental strategies best support those business strategies, and learn how to leverage your culture's strengths while minimizing its weaknesses.

CASES IN POINT

In the following illustrations, leaders can find both some green lights and some caution flags to consider as they establish and evaluate their organizations' leadership development efforts.

Going Overboard

Vanessa is the director of leadership development for a successful manufacturer and retailer of personal care products. She has been with the company from its inception, and the organization's strategy has always been driven by a spirit of innovation and creativity. The company devotes a great deal of its resources to research and development, for instance, and it gives members of the marketing staff the time and freedom to come up with creative approaches to their jobs.

Vanessa's job responsibilities include devising structures for training the retail staff members and outsourcing development programs for the company's managers and executives. In doing so she has always taken into account the company's emphasis on innovation and creativity. She tries to incorporate every new spin on training and leadership development, she is constantly on the lookout for new and better providers of leadership development programs, and she has even instituted an in-house award given to employees who come up with the most innovative sales techniques.

Vanessa has embraced the company's business drivers in her leadership development efforts, and that's commendable. But her approach might have some downsides.

Vanessa's strategy mirrors the value the company places on new ideas. In this organization, people who want to change old habits are encouraged to practice new behaviors, for which they are then recognized. An organizational culture that encourages and recognizes new behaviors goes a long way toward building sustainable leadership capacity.

Such a culture also presents pitfalls for leadership development, however. In an organization that places a high value on anything that is new, things can get old pretty quickly. Vanessa emphasizes the adoption of cutting-edge leadership development practices, but if she constantly changes the company's approach to leadership development to fit whatever is trendy, the developmental efforts could gain a reputation for being flavor-of-the-month. This approach runs the risk of undercutting sustainable leadership capacity.

Driven by Diversity

Wanda is the vice president of human resources for a mineral mining company. The Western state in which the company is based has an increasingly diverse population, but the company's workforce is fairly homogeneous. Before Wanda was hired, the company's executive team, wary of lawsuits, decided to include an appreciation of diversity among the company's core values. Wanda, who has a background in working with diversity issues, has made progress in implementing this value, but one challenge is that the company has a stable workforce without much turnover—some employees have been with the company for more than twenty-five years.

Wanda is working not only to increase the diversity of the company's workforce but also to incorporate the driver of diversity into the company's leadership development efforts. She believes that diversity means not only recognizing the contributions of diverse groups of employees but also ensuring egalitarian treatment of those contributions. One philosophy she has embraced, therefore, is that everyone in the organization, from mine workers to the chief executive officer, is entitled to some type of leadership development. Wanda realizes that not everyone needs the same type of development, so she has created different outlets for different groups of employees. One step she has taken is to ask the older, more experienced employees to attend classes on how to become mentors. Then the highest-potential younger employees are assigned mentors from this group. Wanda has also established specialized training opportunities for minority employees.

The mining company's decision to make diversity one of its business drivers will have an impact on the organization's ability to build sustainable leadership capacity. But there could be negative as well as positive effects.

The notion that everyone deserves some type of leadership development will strengthen the organization by making all employees feel included and valued. The danger in providing different types of leadership development for different groups is that it could prevent the organization from having a common leadership development language and make it difficult for people to relate to one another. Wanda will need to ensure that the different developmental efforts have enough elements in common that they all produce the desired impact at the organizational level.

Profit and Risk

Larry is the director of corporate training and development for a high-tech company that is facing increasing pressure from shareholders to increase profit margins and stock value. In the past the company had always been able to ride out the ups and downs of Wall Street, but the recent downturn in the economy has made it difficult for the organization to maintain its historical profit margins. The company's long-standing reputation for consistently producing above-target results is now in danger. Concerned about the company's vulnerability in the marketplace, the senior management team has dictated that all operational activities be focused on results and directly linked to organizational strategy.

With results now the principal business driver, Larry has had to justify any expenditures on training and leadership development. But Larry believes that the challenge of doing more with less has actually been advantageous because it forced him to take a hard look at the company's training and development programs and link them directly to the business outcomes sought by the organization. This led to a revelation: he realized that the company had not been applying the same strategic intent in its training efforts that it was applying in all other operational areas. This finding prompted him to create a training program that is focused not only on developing employees but also on furthering the company's results-oriented strategy.

The business driver of improving profit margins and results is helping the company stay competitive in the marketplace. But Larry's decision to incorporate the emphasis on the bottom line into the company's leadership development efforts introduces another level of competition that could be detrimental to the building of sustainable leadership capacity. If the imperative of achieving the best results as quickly as possible continues unchecked, it could foster a climate of internal competition. Although a certain amount of such rivalry is desirable, it can have negative consequences if carried too far.

For example, employees who participate in these leadership development experiences may not share what they have learned with their coworkers. They may feel they can gain an advantage over their colleagues by keeping their new insights to themselves. Discouraging the sharing of learning could have a negative impact on the company's profit margins and results. So despite Larry's best intentions, his leadership development strategy could end up working against the company's principal aims.

No Mistakes

Tim is a manager at a long-established retail company that decided three years ago to pursue quality as one of its principal business drivers. The executive board, knowing that the initiative would have to permeate the entire organization to be successful, insisted that all the company's departments had to commit to the effort before the board would support the investments necessary for the undertaking.

Tim is in charge of the quality program, which includes a monthly meeting of all employees at which any instances of compromised quality—and the person or people responsible—are highlighted for everyone to see. During the three years of the initiative, fewer and fewer instances of substandard quality have been reported. So on the surface the program appears to have been a resounding success. But Tim has just now begun to notice a phenomenon that is causing him concern: people aren't reporting mistakes because they are afraid to.

Many organizations have had success with quality initiatives. But such initiatives can have insidious effects on organizational culture and the building of sustainable leadership capacity.

Although the retail company appears to have made great strides in improving quality, Tim now realizes that people have become fearful of making mistakes on the job—and especially of admitting such mistakes. They are afraid they will face humiliation at the monthly meetings. In addition, no one wants to tarnish what appears to be a three-year track record of steady quality improvement by admitting that there is any need for learning.

Improvement cannot come without learning, and one of the foundations of learning is being able to make mistakes—up to a point at least—and to concede them. Mistakes, whether they are your own or others', provide learning opportunities. When employees are discouraged too vigorously from admitting mistakes, learning opportunities are lost and the organization suffers.

A KEY INGREDIENT

Executives who make investments in their organizations' leadership development are sometimes puzzled when they don't get the expected returns on those investments. They could improve their returns by acknowledging that organizational culture plays a vital role in the development of leaders and then factoring organizational culture into their developmental efforts.

First, however, they must be able to recognize their organizational cultures—no easy task because they are so embedded in those cultures. But there are clues to be found.

Ask yourself some questions: What does it *feel* like in your organization? What stories are told over and over in your organization, and what values do those stories promote? What are the drivers of your organization's business strategy, and how have they shaped the organizational culture? Once you have a clearer understanding of your organizational culture, you can pinpoint how it may be hindering or enhancing leadership development efforts in your organization.

Quality Control: Why Leaders Need to Understand Personality

Robert Hogan and Robert B. Kaiser

Every individual has a personality, and because the primary responsibility of managers is dealing with people, it's important for managers to grasp the different types of personality and the implications of each type for the work world. With a clear understanding of how people are alike and the important ways in which they differ, managers are in a strong position to be effective leaders. In particular, knowledge of personality translates into effectiveness in hiring employees, leading employees, and managing yourself.

Managers tend to be pragmatic, and for good reason. They are responsible for managing valuable resources, including time, money, and materials. But the most important resource that managers oversee is people; managers are first and foremost in the people business. It follows then that to perform well, managers need to know something about personality.

Personality involves two main components. The first is human nature—what all people are like, deep inside. The second is individual differences—the important ways in which people differ from one another. Managers who don't understand human nature and individual differences are poorly equipped to motivate people and help them perform. But with a clear understanding of human nature and individual differences, managers are in a strong position to be effective leaders.

The study of personality has a long history. Early societies, from the Chinese in the East to the Greeks in the West, speculated about human nature and human uniqueness. A key lesson from the history of thought about personality is that it is important to start with the right assumptions.

Sigmund Freud was the pioneer of modern personality psychology. Despite his important contributions, he started with the wrong key assumptions—he postulated that the most important generalizations that can be made about people are that everyone is neurotic and that the basic problems of life involve overcoming one's neuroses. Although most people enjoy analyzing themselves, research shows that doing so doesn't provide much guidance for dealing with other people at work, in close relationships, and elsewhere. Moreover, it is simply not true that most people are neurotic.

Business school faculties tend to promote the views of American psychologist Abraham Maslow on personality. Maslow, a humanist, was more concerned with politics than with science. His ideas about self-actualization closely resemble Karl Marx's view that the role of the state is to help each person reach his or her full potential. And just as Marxism has failed as a theory of economics, self-actualization has failed as a theory of personality. After half a century, psychologists are still unable to measure self-actualization. However, the pursuit of self-actualization was a driving force, and often a justification, for much of the self-indulgence and cultural excess of the 1960s, 1970s, and 1980s.

TWO CONDITIONS

A useful view of personality should satisfy two conditions. First, it must be consistent with what is known about human evolution—otherwise it is unlikely to adequately characterize human nature. Second, it must identify the most consequential ways in which people differ—ways that can account for important differences in job performance, career success, relationships, health, and longevity, among other factors.

Human Nature

Taken together, anthropology, sociology, and evolutionary biology provide a view of human nature that centers on a robust generalization with powerful practical implications. Primates are the most social of all the animal families, and human beings are supersocial primates—we evolved living in groups. This fact holds the key to understanding human nature.

Group living was a survival strategy that provided a buffer against harsh elements and powerful predators. Humans have always lived in groups, and this reflects strong needs for social interaction and being a part of something larger than ourselves. Every human group also has a status hierarchy—there are people at the bottom, in the middle, and at the top, and everyone knows who is where. People at the top exert more influence and enjoy more privileges than those below them; consequently, there are real benefits to status. Finally, every human group has a religion that prescribes and justifies its rules regarding acceptable behavior. These rules and belief systems provide guidance and a sense of group identity; they also reduce ambiguity and help people interact, recognize members of their own group, and determine what is valuable.

The fact that group living, status striving, and religion are universal traits among humans suggests that human nature rests on three innate and fundamental needs—*getting along, getting ahead,* and *finding meaning in life.*

Getting along involves gaining social acceptance and avoiding rejection; it is rewarding to be liked and accepted, and stressful to be criticized or rejected. That's why solitary confinement is the most aversive form of punishment.

Getting ahead involves gaining status and respect and avoiding loss of power. Winning a promotion at work or defeating a competitor on the court triggers a pleasurable neurochemical bath of serotonin; losing triggers the release of the stress hormone cortisol.

Finding meaning involves developing a purpose in life that is valued by one's social group; a sense of meaning also provides some degree of structure and predictability in the environment. Those who see no meaning in life are listless and disengaged, and everyone becomes distressed by chaos and a loss of control.

Humans' universal needs to get along, get ahead, and find meaning are rooted in biology—these needs facilitated the survival of our ancestors. Moreover, people with lots of social support, power, and sense of purpose do better today. As super-social creatures, people use social interaction to fulfill these important needs. Much of modern social life takes place at work, among other organizational settings, and therefore the workplace provides opportunities to gain acceptance, increase one's status and power, and identify with a larger group and its purpose. These three needs provide managers with their most important levers for motivating people.

Individual Differences

Not all people are equally skilled at getting along, getting ahead, and finding meaning. People differ in their ability to meet these needs, and these differences are reflected in their values, beliefs, dispositions, talents, and typical behaviors. This is what we mean by the term personality.

It is useful to distinguish between *personality from the inside* and *personality from the outside*. Personality from the inside entails how people think about themselves—their hopes, dreams, goals, fears, and strategies for getting along, getting ahead, and finding meaning; these self-views form a person's *identity*. Personality from the outside entails how other people think about a particular person, which is that person's *reputation*—the things others need to know in order to be able to deal with that person effectively.

Identity is *the you that you know* and reputation is *the you that others know*. These two forms of personality are different in important ways. Freud said that the you that you know is hardly worth knowing because you made it all up. He was partially right;

for example, there is typically little correspondence between self-ratings and coworker ratings in 360-degree feedback. Nonetheless, identity is important because it *explains* why people do what they do, even if their behavior, and the reasons they give for it, make little sense to observers.

Individuals' reputations determine how others interact with them; for example, if others think that an individual is overly critical, they will tend to avoid him or her. Reputation is a summary of how individuals have behaved in the past and is the best information available about how they are likely to behave in the future—because the best predictor of future behavior is past behavior. Reputation determines some of the most consequential outcomes in life: it is the basis on which people are promoted, married, collaborated with, loaned money, and liked or despised.

There are two distinct aspects of reputation—the *bright side* and the *dark side*. The bright side reflects individuals' social performance when they are at their best. The dark side reflects individuals' social performance when they let their guard down—when they are stressed out, overworked, or simply do not care what kind of an impression they make. The bright side describes the person met in an employment interview; the dark side describes the person evaluated at the end of the year.

Researchers have identified five basic dimensions that form the bright side of personality; they are known as the *Big Five*. These dimensions are *adjustment, extraversion, likeability, prudence,* and *openness*, and they reflect the common terms that people use to describe other people in the early stages of a relationship. All people describe and compare one another in terms of these five dimensions.

Adjustment involves poise and self-confidence, a key ingredient for success in both getting along and getting ahead. Extraversion splits into two components, sociability and ambition, that seem similar but serve different needs. Sociability involves being affable and outgoing, which is important for getting along. Ambition involves competitive status seeking and directly concerns getting ahead. Likeability is about being considerate and congenial and is a key factor in getting along. Prudence involves following rules and working hard, which are related to both getting along and getting ahead. Openness is the key to creativity and includes seeming curious and intellectually engaged, which facilitates finding meaning.

The role of the Big Five in job performance has been widely studied and there is substantial data indicating that they predict job performance at every level in every organization.

Dark-side tendencies typically coexist with well-developed social skills, which mask or compensate for the dark-side tendencies in the short run. Over time, however, as we get to know people better, their dark-side tendencies emerge. The dark side concerns behavioral tendencies associated with getting along and getting ahead that can be effective in the near term. For example, arrogant people may at first seem poised and self-confident. However, dark-side tendencies rest on flawed assumptions about one's capabilities and others' reactions (for instance, "There is nothing I can't do!" or, "Other people find me irresistible"), and these flawed assumptions and their associated behaviors tend to undermine relationships in the long term. In many ways the dark side can be understood as a set of otherwise attractive qualities that are overdone; for example, confidence turns into arrogance, creativity becomes eccentricity, tact becomes sucking up, and so on.

Psychologists have identified eleven counterproductive dimensions of personality that constitute the dark side—*excitable, skeptical, cautious, reserved, leisurely, bold, mischievous, colorful, imaginative, diligent,* and *dutiful.* There is less research on the effects of the dark side at work than there is on the bright side effects. However, although some of the dark-side dimensions may at first glance appear to be tendencies that are desirable in managers, they have been linked to long-term weaknesses that lead to poor judgment, bad leadership, and derailment. Moreover, everyone has at least some of these tendencies, so career development depends on coming to terms with them.

WHAT IT MEANS

What we have discussed so far is an overview of personality at the conceptual level. These concepts have wide-ranging, practical implications for managers, notably in the areas of *hiring employees, leading employees,* and *managing yourself.*

Hiring Employees

Over the past twenty years, researchers have found overwhelming evidence that personality inventories based on the Big Five predict performance in every job in the U.S. economy. However, different jobs require different personality characteristics. For example, research shows that good long-distance truck drivers are not particularly sociable or ambitious but are very prudent. Conversely, good salespeople are highly sociable and ambitious but not very prudent. Careful analysis of performance requirements can identify the configuration of personality characteristics suited for a given job.

Personality inventories are particularly useful for identifying leadership potential. Research shows that the Big Five predict leadership better than IQ does. Effective leaders are adjusted (optimistic and calm under pressure), ambitious (driven and competitive), sociable (energetic and communicative), prudent (hard working and industrious), open (visionary and eager to learn), and somewhat likeable (agreeable but also objective and tough-minded).

Assessing the dark side of personality is also helpful in selection. Because well-developed social skills usually mask dark-side tendencies in the short run, these destructive tendencies are hard to detect using bright-side measures, interviews, or assessment centers. However, a measure of the dark side can help hiring managers determine when self-confident applicants are actually arrogant or when attention to detail may be a sign of micromanagement. Ironically, many derailed managers were fired for the same reasons they were hired—their strengths became weaknesses, as CCL researchers have put it.

Competent personality measures have two distinct advantages as selection devices. First, they predict performance quite well. Second, unlike IQ tests, personality measures do not discriminate against any protected category of job applicants—minority applicants and women achieve similar scores to majority applicants and men. It is also worth mentioning that the claim that personality inventories can be deceived is simply false. It is one thing to fake an answer to a single item—for instance, "I have never told a lie"—but it is impossible to manufacture a fake profile on a multidimensional inventory.

Leading Employees

We have noted that the universal needs to get along, get ahead, and find meaning provide the most important levers for motivating people. Employees perform better when they have positive relationships with their managers and coworkers, a sense of community, and protection from bullying and harassment. Employees also want a good income, opportunities for advancement, freedom to decide how to do their work, and a clear vision from their leaders to give their work meaning and purpose. Effective managers have the skills to fulfill these needs for their employees.

Personality is also about individual differences, which means that people vary in their degree of motivation to fulfill their needs to get along, get ahead, and find meaning. Savvy managers understand these differences. For example, ambitious employees want opportunities to take on leadership roles, demonstrate their competence, and earn bonuses and other forms of recognition. Employees who are low in ambition, however, find extra responsibilities and challenging assignments stressful. Employees who are highly likeable are concerned about peaceful relations at work and being accepted by their coworkers; employees with low likeability are comfortable with conflict and dislike working on teams.

Prudent employees need clear rules and a structured environment, whereas employees low in prudence find structure stifling. Employees low on adjustment need a lot of reassurance, find criticism very stressful, and ignore positive feedback; employees high on adjustment need no reassurance and ignore criticism. These examples make the point that sophisticated managers tailor their methods to the personalities of the individuals being managed.

A knowledge of personality is indispensable for leading teams. Research shows clearly that there are *team player* personalities and *team killer* personalities. The best-performing teams are composed of people high on adjustment, likeability, and prudence—team players are even-tempered, cooperative, and conforming. Team killers are moody, quarrelsome, and independent. Moreover, the old adage about one bad apple pertains to teams: research shows that it takes only one person who is low on adjustment, likeability, and prudence to degrade the performance of the whole team.

Effective teams are also characterized by a range of complementary skills, perspectives, and talents. The biggest challenge is to find the right mix of people to play the various roles needed for a high-performing team. Most models of team composition stress the importance of four roles tied to personality—*leadership, production, problem solving,* and *relationship maintenance*. Leadership roles are best played by ambitious employees who want to coordinate and guide the team's work. Production roles need prudent employees who are good at implementation and driving tasks to completion. Problem solving depends on employees with high scores for openness. Finally, the crucial role of relationship maintenance requires likeable and sociable people who are good at building cohesion and facilitating communication.

The diversity of a team produces a second challenge—establishing trust and respect among the different personalities. Creating an atmosphere of trust is the central task of the leader, who needs to understand and respect the unique contributions of different approaches, emphasize collective goals and shared fate, and point out how cooperation leads to better performance than does competition.

Managing Yourself

Being able to manage yourself is at least as important for your career as being able to manage others. Self-management begins with self-awareness, which means understanding your personality. This is complicated by the fact that individuals inevitably think of themselves differently from how other people view them. The you that you know can be thought of as the protagonist in your internal narrative who makes sense of the world. However, you are merely part of the supporting cast—or perhaps even an antagonist—in other people's internal narratives.

It is interesting to note that derailed managers are often described as self-absorbed. This suggests that they are unaware of how they are perceived by others. The data suggest that successful managers do understand how they are perceived by others and are skilled at creating a favorable reputation.

Managers can use self-awareness in two ways to better manage themselves. First, they need to know their natural tendencies—the types of activities they gravitate toward and are good at and also the activities they tend to avoid. For instance, a manager high in openness but low in prudence is likely to be creative and to see possibilities that others overlook. Such a manager is well suited for strategic leadership but is also unlikely to be good with the details of implementation and tactical problem solving. To be effective this manager will need to put extra effort into developing operational leadership skills or will need to hire and empower a team member with a complementary profile to fulfill the operational roles.

Second, managers must understand their dark-side tendencies and the kinds of situations that provoke those behaviors. This is particularly difficult because dark-side tendencies rest on flawed, self-serving assumptions. One's best bet is to take a dark-side personality assessment and muster the courage to review the results honestly. It is also helpful to get coworker feedback on how one's dark side plays out. Then, using this information and perhaps working with a coach, managers can develop strategies and tactics for managing the potentially disruptive effects of their dark sides.

Ignorance may be bliss in some situations, but in the case of the dark side, ignorance is a lethal career strategy.

A Key Link in the Chain

Maxine A. Dalton

The responsibility for development lies squarely on the shoulders of the person seeking development. This does not, however, diminish the critical role of that person's manager, who is a crucial link in the development process. Those who design and implement development programs need to help managers understand what roles they must play and how to play them.

Managers must provide developmental experiences, support and feedback, and access to organizational resources. In short, managers play a critical role in making development count for their direct reports and their organizations. Managers are in a position to know what work needs to be done and how the direct report's development can contribute. They are the critical element that can connect development to business results.

But managers sometimes fail in this task because development is often thought of as "training," which gives rise to doubts that it will have a substantial effect on business results or even on the direct reports themselves. By demanding that development plans have a clear relation to the work of the organization, however, managers can make development real and communicate to their direct reports that development is important.

An individual's development depends on experiences, and the manager plays the most direct role in determining which experiences the direct report will have. As the experience gatekeeper, the manager can open the door to new tasks, interactions with new people, and new business ventures. The manager can also, sometimes unwittingly, prevent the direct report from having developmental experiences.

The manager usually has a hand in deciding which new job assignments a direct report will get, but development often must take place in the context of the direct report's current role, without a change in jobs. The manager needs to view the direct report's current assignment as an important source of learning opportunities and must find ways to help the direct report use these opportunities.

Managers must be shown how to see the developmental challenge in every assignment and how to coach for task and process outcomes. A direct report who is given the task of turning around sales, for instance, can also use that opportunity to learn how to delegate more effectively.

The process of development is really about teaching others how to learn. If managers are oriented toward identifying and benefiting from the challenges embedded in every opportunity, those being developed will follow suit. Human resource departments need to help managers assume a framework in which day-to-day work experiences are viewed as learning opportunities that can be coordinated with development plans.

Developmental opportunities abound in most organizations. Managers with the reputation of being "people developers" know where the opportunities are and how to access them. They know what organizational support is available and how to influence decisions about assignments so that both the direct report and the organization will profit.

Learning new skills is seldom easy, and feedback is a crucial part of the process—but it can't be a one-shot deal. The manager often is in the best position to provide the necessary support and ongoing feedback to the direct report. Most individuals who benefit from development programs have managers who care—who take the time and have the skills to provide support and feedback.

Launching a development program requires bringing on board the managers who will serve these primary roles in development. Unless managers understand the importance and duties of their roles and unless they buy into the program, results are likely to be sketchy at best.

But many managers have never thought of their development roles so specifically. They haven't thought about how critical their task is, the dynamics of development, or how to access organizational resources. They may not have the planning, support, and feedback skills required to be effective in their roles.

The main task then, for those who design and implement development programs, is to educate managers in all these areas.

Character Study: Strengthening the Heart of Good Leadership

Gene Klann

In recent years, headlines in the business pages have underscored the fact that some corporate leaders leave a lot to be desired in the area of character. Yet because it is subjective and controversial, the issue of character has largely been left out of the equation when it comes to training and preparing leaders. If undertaken with the right perspective, however, there are ways to develop character in leaders.

Some leaders are convinced that they live by their reputations. For them the way they are viewed by others is not the most important thing—it's the only thing. But as scandals in the corporate world in the early part of this millennium made clear, reputation carries a leader only so far. It needs substance to back it up. Senior executives at companies such as Enron, ImClone, Tyco, and WorldCom were riding high on their images and their purported records of performance before reality spoiled the party. Events might have turned out far differently for these leaders if they had heeded the advice of legendary UCLA basketball coach John Wooden: "Be more concerned with your character than your reputation, because your character is what you really are, while your reputation is merely what others think you are."

Especially in a military context, character's place as an essential trait of effective leaders has long been recognized and acknowledged. Edgar F. Puryear Jr., in his book *American Generalship* (subtitled *Character Is Everything: The Art of Command*) (Presidio Press, 2000), writes that "the greatest personal quality of all is character, which is everything in leadership. . . . From my research . . . it is clear that there is absolutely nothing as important in successful leadership as character. Many great generals, such as George Washington, Robert E. Lee, and George C. Marshall, are remembered not only as great leaders but also as men whose character predominated."

Lee, in particular, is regarded by history as a military leader of exceptionally strong character. In the wake of the Civil War,

it was Lee's leadership by example that promoted reconciliation, rebuilding, and national harmony and discouraged those who wanted to resume the fight against the Union.

The role of character in effective leadership has also been recognized in the business world, although perhaps not on the scale that it has been in the military realm. Most people know intuitively that good character helps people reach their full potential and achieve success; increases productivity; enhances self-acceptance, self-confidence, energy, and enthusiasm; and improves interpersonal relationships. And the issue of character in corporate leaders has risen to the forefront in recent years as a number of widely publicized cases of character meltdown (or of bad character surfacing) among highly visible leaders resulted in significant damage to their organizations. It has become evident that character deficiencies in business leaders can have dire consequences in terms of financial losses, litigation, government scrutiny, employee morale and retention, company reputation, and public confidence.

Yet even though the importance of character in leaders is generally acknowledged in the business world, the understanding and development of character have been largely ignored by business schools and other institutions that train leaders and by organizations themselves. There are a number of reasons for this, but the principal one is that ideas about character—and associated concepts such as morality, ethics, and integrity—are inherently subjective and thus controversial. Implicit in the notion of character is that there are right and wrong standards of behavior. But on what are those standards based, and who determines them? Are they based on some natural order of things, on societal or cultural norms, on what the individual alone believes to be right and wrong, on a set of divine directives, or on some combination of these? Also, in Western societies that emphasize humanism and individualism, there is a natural resistance to character standards and moral codes that may be viewed as narrow-minded, intolerant, and restrictive of freedom of choice and action. In addition, some elements of character may be perceived as mutually exclusive: both *boldness* and *cautiousness* are often described as good character qualities, for instance, as are *action orientation* and *patience.* Considering all this, it's not hard to understand why most business schools and organizations have shied away from programs designed to promote character development.

Character development in organizations is generally limited to defining appropriate and inappropriate behaviors in relation to specific areas such as sexual harassment, diversity, and affirmative action and to providing sensitivity training. Defining and instilling behaviors and attitudes relating to broad moral and ethical choices are largely disregarded. Most organizations have drawn up a statement of values, but in many cases this statement is largely for show and is given little more than lip service. The fact is that what many companies and many of their leaders continue to value most is the bottom line—profit margins, shareholder value, and the like. In the consuming drive to climb the corporate ladder, leaders often compromise character to reach performance goals, forgetting that enduring, positive influence depends on the type of people they are, not merely on power, titles, and personal wealth. Also, there is a widespread but mistaken belief that an individual's character is totally and indelibly determined at an early age, so efforts to develop character in adults are often seen as a waste of time.

Despite these barriers, there are steps that leaders can take to develop character in themselves and others in their organizations, using as a basis for such development the judicious application of the laws of the land, the values and standards of the organization, and the social acceptability of any given conduct.

WHO'S LOOKING

What is character? The word is commonly used but difficult to define.

Webster's II New College Dictionary has nineteen entries under *character*, as a noun, adjective, and transitive verb. Its core meaning as a noun is "the combination of emotional, intellectual, and moral qualities that distinguishes a person." Derived from the Greek *kharassein* ("to inscribe"), the word can vary in meaning according to its usage. For instance, if someone does something unexpected, people may describe the behavior as being *out of character*. In the legal world, defense lawyers may ask their clients to obtain *character references* from reputable friends to help their cases in court. And in the movie business, people who are adept at playing specific types of supporting roles are known as *character actors*. One particularly incisive definition of character comes from H. Jackson Brown Jr., author of *Life's Little Instruction Book: 511 Suggestions, Observations, and Reminders on How to Live a Happy and Rewarding Life* (Thomas Nelson, 1991), who writes that "character is what we do when we think no one is looking."

In a leadership context, character is an individual's pattern of behavior that indicates his or her moral strength, fortitude, and selflessness. (The key phrase is "pattern of behavior.") A leader's moral strength relates to his or her concepts of right and wrong and motivation to live by those beliefs. Fortitude is a leader's courage and determination to do what he or she believes is right regardless of the consequences, to take a stand and refuse to compromise that belief system in spite of pressures to do so. And selflessness is the leader's ability to put others, the organization, the community, and society before self-interest and personal gain. Viewed in this way, character can be compared to the heart. A person can function with a malfunctioning or weak heart but not very well and not for long. The same is true of a leader with a flawed or feeble character.

The foundation of an individual's character is formed from experiences and influences in childhood and adolescence—from home life, schooling, interactions with peers, religious upbringing or lack thereof, and other factors. These contacts and exposures largely determine people's later patterns of behavior—their concepts of right and wrong, personal moral codes, and value systems. Feedback, in the form of rewards and sanctions, also plays a major role in shaping and adjusting an individual's early pattern of behavior—and thus his or her character.

But character development does not—or at least should not—stop when an individual reaches adulthood. Like intellectual, physical, and spiritual development, character development should be a continuous, lifelong process. This is especially true for leaders, who as they move into positions of increased responsibility are faced with new and heightened challenges to their character. As leaders are confronted with mounting pressures (for instance, to deliver results at any cost even if doing so requires violating their moral code or value system), they need to constantly reassess, refine, and validate their patterns of behavior. People tend to show their true colors when they are under pressure, so leaders should focus on building character that they can display consistently, even through the inevitable stressful times.

Character comes into play when leaders must respond to moral and ethical choices. In such situations, leaders are presented with a number of options—options that may be filled with ambiguity. For instance, one choice may conform with societal, cultural, or organizational rules and standards of behavior, another may not, and a third may be open to interpretation. Sometimes there are no clear-cut right and wrong options, and arguments can be made on both sides of each possible choice. In any case, when a leader is required to make such choices, his or her character will largely determine the choices ultimately made.

For these reasons one of the key responsibilities of leaders is to establish an effective process of character development—not only for themselves but also for their subordinates.

THE FIVE E'S

How can a process be established by which leaders can develop not only their own character but also the character of their subordinates in the line of succession? The system I propose comprises five elements that could be called the five E's: *example, education, environment, experience,* and *evaluation.*

Example

Leadership by example is the ability to influence others through actions and attitudes. It is a powerful way to develop character because it leverages the natural human tendency to emulate the behavior of individuals held in high esteem. People like to model themselves after those who have power and authority, who are successful and respected. Leaders' behavior sets the standard for the entire organization—others learn from their actions, words, and attitudes.

In one sense, leaders are conducting a perpetual leadership clinic. That's why it's essential that they display a pattern of behavior—a character—that is worthy of imitation. Behaviors that leaders should practice to set the right example include being decisive, confronting and publicly discussing the ethics involved in tough issues, promoting diversity, advocating risk taking, creating a feedback-rich environment, being visible, and listening.

Education

Organizations can set up formal and informal training that focuses on the importance of character, the potential pressures on and challenges to character resulting from such things as performance expectations and market competition, and the short- and long-term implications of a lapse of character.

Leaders from various levels of the organization should take part in the training. This puts them all on the same page and gives them a shared frame of reference. The organization's culture and its value system can be used in the training as guidelines for actions and behavior that reflect good character. This approach has the added advantage of revealing whether the culture and values are still practical, realistic, and current.

Senior leaders should be the facilitators for at least some of the discussions about moral and ethical choices. By sharing the experiences and influences that formed and reinforced their patterns of behavior, senior leaders can engage in a dialogue about character with the organization's emerging leaders. They can also lessen the chances that they themselves will fall victim to character lapses, because it is highly motivational when leaders know that others have them under the microscope to see whether they practice what they preach.

Another way for organizations and leaders to promote character development is through self-education. When leaders know that they have a personal responsibility to enhance their knowledge of subjects such as integrity, morality, and ethics, it can result in greater motivation, retention, and practical application than if the character training is taught by others. One way that organizations can support character self-education is by establishing an in-house library of relevant books, articles, and video- and audiotapes.

Environment

An organization's environment plays a huge role in determining whether the character development of leaders is encouraged or impeded. The environment is essentially the organization's culture—its collective personality, attitudes, and outlook—and the culture is shaped and developed over time by the actions and values of people in the organization.

Most organizations evolve patterns of behavior that are promoted, recognized, and rewarded—and thus are expected of their leaders. If these behaviors are positive, if they promote the general good, chances are that the organization can implement an effective character development process. However, when character is not emphasized over factors such as profit in the behaviors that are desired and valued, the message sent is clear: the organization places priority on qualities other than character and thus has little interest in character development.

Senior leaders can establish an environment that is open to character development by creating a clear, detailed, practical set of organizational values and by ensuring that everyone in the organization lives those values rather than just goes through the motions. This set of values—those things that the organization considers important, useful, and admirable—will be more relevant and more likely to be accepted and followed if it is generated with input from all levels of the organization. If the value set emphasizes positive behaviors and traits, it can be an important benchmark for character development and can help keep leaders within the ethical and moral boundaries of the organization. It will be of little use, however, without clearly understood and enforced disciplinary consequences for violations of those boundaries at all levels of the organization.

Experience

A key element of the U.S. Army's leadership development model is experiential—giving officers challenging assignments that because of the responsibilities and risks associated with them are highly developmental. In the business world as well, some jobs and assignments are extremely challenging and carry great responsibility, whereas others are more routine. The former are more likely to enhance character development.

In view of this outcome, senior leaders should ensure that as part of the overall development process, high-potential employees are given "stretch" positions and assignments requiring them to make difficult choices, which can help them better understand and develop character. Such positions and assignments might relate to corporate tactics and strategy, quality control, customer relations, budgeting, production efficiency, and employee safety. These types of jobs not only challenge high potentials and provide an environment conducive to character development but also give senior leaders good indications of the character strengths and weaknesses of those who might become the future leaders of the organization.

Evaluation

Ongoing feedback is a key element of any developmental experience, and character development is no exception. Feedback provides information that lets leaders know how their character measures up and how they are progressing toward their character development goals. For feedback to be effective, however, senior leaders first need to establish and communicate to their subordinates clear expectations regarding patterns of behavior; when these expectations are not provided, it's the responsibility of the junior leaders to seek them out. Once the expectations are established as a road map for character development, leaders can have quarterly feedback sessions with their bosses to gauge their progress, reviewing specific instances when their character was challenged and either stood fast or cracked. Organizations can also add sections on integrity, ethics, adherence to values, and other character-related behaviors to their performance evaluation forms. In addition, leaders can self-assess their character-development progress by answering a checklist of questions that encourages them to examine whether they currently possess the right motivation, mind-set, and tools to support their character development.

RIGHT CHOICES

The character-development process described in this article is helpful and practical but certainly not the final answer. Nor are the leaders who might find this system useful perfect human beings—they inevitably make mistakes and bad choices. The key is the ability to determine the difference between right and wrong, good and bad, moral and immoral. Leaders who have this ability may not always make the right, good, and moral choice, but at least they are aware of the alternative. If they focus on an ongoing process of developing and maintaining character, they'll improve their chances of choosing that alternative in the future.

A Retention Strategy for the Ages

Karen Bryson and Karissa McKenna

Leaders who think that the current employment climate means the job of keeping key talent can be put on the back burner might want to think again. Demographics show that retention will become increasingly critical and challenging in the years ahead. Knowing what baby boomers and Generation Xers need and want in the workplace can provide an advantage in the battle for talent.

It is human nature to categorize and place labels on groups of people, and nowhere is this truer than in comparisons of and relations between generations. To take just one example, it seems that every generation admonishes the one that follows with the old line, "When I was growing up . . . ," and is dismissed by that ensuing generation as a bunch of old fogies.

Few would dispute that there are marked generational gaps. Values, philosophies, outlooks, moods, attitudes, abilities, interests, work ethics, and especially cultural tastes—in music, fashion, hairstyles, and the like—can vary substantially from generation to generation. (Bill Cosby once observed that "nothing separates the generations more than music.")

But at the core of human existence—what people truly need and want—are the variances among generations really so pronounced? What specific things do individuals from different generations need and want, and what can be done to provide them with those things? These are important questions for leaders to consider in developing and managing a multigenerational workforce and preparing for the futures of their organizations.

Perhaps the main reason why leaders need to be aware of generational differences is retention—winning the battle for key talent, creating enough stability in the workforce to make an organization effective and successful, and maintaining and developing a sufficient number of high-potential employees in the leadership pipeline. Employers who understand and respond to the needs and desires of their talented employees from each generation are much more likely to retain and motivate those key people. The economic downturn that is now headed into its third year may have tempted some leaders to put the issue of retention on the back burner, but it remains a critical challenge—for a number of reasons.

Despite the thousands of layoffs of the past couple of years, many organizations are struggling to find skilled people who can fill important roles and add strategic value at all levels. And a demographic trend suggests the need for qualified employees will grow considerably in the next ten to twenty years, as the pool of available talent shrinks rapidly.

The two groups that dominate the current ranks of the employed are the Baby Boom generation (here defined as those born between 1946 and 1963) and Generation X (those born between 1964 and 1983). The majority of today's leaders in corporate America are boomers, but Gen Xers are emerging as leaders and are expected to shoulder the brunt of the leadership responsibilities soon—in some cases, sooner than they might think.

The oldest boomers are in their mid-sixties and have reached or are close to reaching retirement age. Many boomers who achieved top leadership positions have already retired or are planning to soon. To determine what this means in terms of the retention and succession challenges facing organizations, the math is simple—and the numbers don't lie. Generation X is one of the smallest generations in U.S. history; there are seventy-six million boomers in the current workforce but only sixty-six million Gen-Xers.

The impending wave of boomer retirements, combined with the deficit in qualified Gen Xers to take those boomers' places, will ripple through the economy. Candidates with the right skills will be in even higher demand than presently, and organizations will have to scramble even harder to fill key positions. This phenomenon is already being felt, especially in the upper echelons, as recent business surveys show that many organizations have experienced significant challenges in filling their top leadership positions or are projecting that they will do so in the next five years. Increases in executive turnover, along with the move toward flatter organizations that leave less room for developing high-potential individuals, are exacerbating the problem.

Even when organizations are able to find qualified people from outside to replace those who have left for other organizations or retired, they pay a dear price. It's estimated that the costs related to replacing an employee—for recruiting, selection, training, loss of productivity during the vacancy, and so forth—amount to 150 percent of the previous employee's annual salary and benefits package. To replace someone in a management or sales position, the costs are estimated to range up to 250 percent of the previous employee's compensation package.

DEFINING THE CHALLENGE

It is clear that for organizations to sustain success over the next twenty years, they need to concentrate on attracting and retaining as many high-quality employees as possible. But to ensure a competitive edge, organizations also must focus on developing more of these people and placing them in the leadership pipeline so they will be prepared for the challenges ahead in an increasingly complex business environment.

To achieve these goals of recruitment, retention, development, and succession planning, leaders need to understand the generations with which they are dealing. They need to be aware not so much of superficial differences such as tastes in music and fashion as of differences in the core characteristics that form a generation's personality—what makes the members of that generation tick, their values and ideals, and most of all what they need and want in the workplace. Leaders who know and use this information have the best chance of not only keeping but also engaging and motivating their most talented and highest-potential people.

But how can leaders know what a Gen Xer employee, for instance, needs and wants and how that might differ from the needs and desires of a boomer employee? Leaders might be tempted to rely on stereotypes or instinct, but those approaches aren't likely to get them very far.

WHAT THEY WANT

Seeking to find out what organizations and leaders need to do to keep their key people from the two predominant working generations, Generation X and baby boomer, CCL conducted a study as part of its Emerging Leaders Research Project. The results offer a valuable tool for organizations that want to do all they can to retain their key talent for the challenging times ahead. The data also might come as a surprise to those who would expect to find significant differences between the factors important to retaining members of the two generations. The seven major retention themes mentioned most often by the survey respondents—compensation, challenge, support, advancement, recognition, values, and organizational success—were mentioned with similar frequency by both boomers and Gen Xers. Following is a look at what the two generations say about what it takes to keep them as committed members of their organizations, and what leaders and organizations can do to respond to these employees' needs and desires.

Compensation

Compensation was the factor mentioned most often by both boomers and Gen Xers when discussing what it would take to keep them as committed employees. It was also the area in which the two generations differed most in the frequency with which they mentioned a retention factor—close to half of the Gen Xers cited it compared with about one-third of the boomers.

The respondents' descriptions of compensation encompassed not only pay and other monetary rewards but also benefits, including job flexibility. However, the respondents' focus was on monetary compensation, with most of them saying it was important that it be fair, based on merit, and increased over time. Job flexibility was the second most mentioned compensation topic, with many respondents specifying that they wanted a flexible work schedule or the option of telecommuting.

Even armed with the knowledge that compensation is a key retention factor, leaders don't always have a lot of leeway to provide higher salaries to the people they want to keep. When that's the case, it's critical that leaders be honest with themselves and with the employees about what the organization can and cannot provide.

The study results suggest that the most important thing is that the compensation structure be competitive in the marketplace, fair, and based on merit—and that the employees view it as such. (It may be helpful for leaders to provide employees with information about the compensation structure and the organization's philosophy on compensation.) If the organization's compensation structure does not meet those three criteria, some key people will inevitably choose to go elsewhere.

At the same time, leaders should keep in mind that there are types of compensation other than pay. Talented employees' dissatisfaction with their salaries may be assuaged with better health benefits, more paid time off, or greater job flexibility. Or these employees might be convinced to stay if the leader and the organization are outstanding at one of the other retention factors, such as advancement and career planning, support and development, or recognition of employee efforts.

Challenge

Both boomers and Gen Xers frequently mentioned their desire to be challenged in their work. Many of them placed a priority on having duties that motivate and interest them, on having their talents fully employed, and on being given opportunities to grow. Boomers brought up this theme less often than Gen Xers did, but that was mainly because only 26 percent of male boomers described challenge as a major retention factor for them. Among female boomers and all Gen Xers, about four in ten mentioned challenge.

The results suggest that challenge is an important way to keep people with the organization, motivate them, develop them, and enable them to contribute to the organization. One tactic leaders can use is to *ask* their employees how they would like to be challenged, what skills would help them meet those challenges, and what support they need to be successful. Then leaders can look for opportunities that align with the answers to those questions. Leaders should also help employees understand how challenges can develop them and prepare them for advancement.

Support

One-third of the Gen Xers and one-fourth of the boomers saw support as an important retention factor. These respondents were concerned specifically with having adequate resources, a reasonable workload, mentoring, training and development, opportunities to learn, and feedback.

Providing a staff with the support it needs to do its work effectively, learn, and develop is key to the success of not only individual employees but of the entire organization. Leaders should do a thorough assessment of the support offered to employees—evaluating physical resources as well as opportunities for development, formal or informal mentoring, and feedback. Once leaders have an accurate idea of the support that is in place, they can look for ways to maximize that support. Possibilities include offering days off to attend conferences, opportunities to work with or observe someone in another department or at a higher level, and tuition reimbursement. In any case, development plans and learning opportunities should be clear and integrated in performance systems.

Advancement

Here's where boomers and Gen Xers were closest in their responses, as nearly one-third of both groups saw opportunities for advancement as a key to their retention. (Interestingly, however, only 18 percent of female boomers mentioned this factor.) Respondents specifically cited opportunities for promotion, professional growth, increased responsibility and influence, and career path planning.

Even though many boomers and Gen Xers view opportunities for advancement as an important retention factor, few of the respondents indicated that they expected immediate promotions. So leaders probably don't have to go out and promote on the spot everyone they want to keep in the organization. But they can score a lot of points in this area by having frank discussions with employees about career paths available in the organization, assessing with each employee where he or she is on a career path and helping that employee plan and prepare for future opportunities.

Recognition

This was one of only two retention themes that boomers named more often than Gen Xers did. It was mentioned most often by female boomers, 43 percent of whom cited it. Respondents talked about receiving respect and understanding, feeling that they are valued, and being able to make significant contributions to the organization and to have those contributions acknowledged.

For leaders, meeting employees' need to be recognized can be as simple as taking the time to do it. Whenever possible, leaders should walk around the workplace and talk with employees just to find out what they're doing. It's important not to micromanage, but it's equally important to recognize when employees are doing a good job and to acknowledge their contributions to the organization.

Values

About two in ten respondents from both generations believed the values of their organization and their leaders to be a significant factor in retention. They talked about specific values they wanted in their organization and workplace, such as fairness, commitment, caring, trust, and stability. Values also encompassed ethics, standards, and morale.

The good news for leaders is that establishing a set of values for both themselves and their organizations doesn't cost anything. But integrating values into the fiber of an organization's culture can be difficult. Nevertheless, there are steps leaders can take to instill values, such as having open discussions with employees about the organization's values and the employees' own values, and the ways the two connect. This can lead to an agreement on what it means to live these values in the workplace and how everyone can support this goal.

Organizational Success

Respondents who cited this important retention factor wanted their organizations to be successful and profitable. Some respondents talked about accomplishing specific goals or implementing certain changes if necessary. Respondents also wanted their organizations to have effective and successful leadership. Organizational success was mentioned more frequently by Gen Xers than by boomers.

Organizational success is clearly related to workplace morale—people naturally want to feel that they are part of a winning team. Many employees also recognize that organizational success is linked to other retention factors; an organization's ability to provide competitive pay and opportunities for advancement, for instance, depends largely on its financial well-being.

Aside from taking the tactical and strategic steps necessary to ensure the success of the business, leaders can underscore organizational success by celebrating company milestones and achievement of goals.

BE HONEST

In today's fast-changing and increasingly complex and competitive business environment, retaining key talent is important to not only organizational success but also survival. Demographics make it clear that retention will become even more critical in the years ahead. Yet retention alone is not enough; organizations also need to motivate and develop their key talent. Luckily, retention strategies also reinforce motivation and development.

Knowing what members of both the current generation of leaders and the generation of emerging leaders want and need to stay with their organizations can help leaders in devising effective retention plans. Moreover, CCL's research suggests that what is important to boomers and Gen Xers may not be so different after all. In the final analysis the biggest key to retention is honest and open communication about what employees need and want and about what the organization can and cannot provide.

Finding Success at Succession

David Berke

In recent years, succession planning—which aims to ensure continuity in key leadership and management functions—has become increasingly important for organizations. There are many reasons for this, but perhaps the most obvious is demographics. The oldest of the baby boomers have reached retirement age, and the group following the boomers, Generation X, is not large enough to replace them.

Demographics, however, are not the only reason why organizations and their leaders should pay attention to succession.

Turnover at the CEO level has grown substantially. According to Bloomberg, the CEO turnover rate in 2011 was at 13 percent, the highest in the past six years. And when a CEO leaves, it is not unusual to see change occur at the next levels of the organization.

Mergers and downsizing in the 1990s stripped out middle-manager positions—traditionally the place where future executives were identified and developed skills, company knowledge, and contacts. And finally, the emphasis on growth in the 1990s may have led companies to focus on hiring from the outside rather than on developing people they already employed to ensure a sufficient pool of candidates.

There is no one best succession planning approach; too much depends on the specifics of a company, its culture, and its business situation. Let's examine two common approaches to succession planning and the lessons that can be drawn from each.

FOLLOW THE LEADER

A common response to the need for succession planning is to find a successful program and copy it. The system that Jack Welch used at General Electric is very popular—and with good reason. But copying it is a poor idea unless your company has a corporate culture, resources, and support systems that are very similar to GE's, not to mention a CEO who is willing to dedicate the time and attention to succession planning that Welch apparently did.

A succession planning system must be built to fit the organization in which it will operate. It should reflect corporate elements that are highly specific to the organization, such as strategy and culture.

Different strategies require managers and executives to have different skill sets. One thing is clear, however: to devise an effective succession planning system, leaders must know where the company is going—or at the very least its likely direction as described in the strategic plan—and what types of resources it has. The greater the uncertainty in the environment, the greater the argument for developing a diverse talent pool, one that can meet both anticipated and unanticipated needs.

As for culture, although it has many elements, there are three that are the most important for succession planning:

- The extent to which the CEO is willing to own the outcomes of the succession planning process
- The organizational philosophy of development and the extent to which development is supported with resources, both of money and people
- The viability of the performance management system, which can provide useful data for managing development and movement

Other questions that must be answered within the context of the organization concern the goals of the desired system and the status of systems to support implementation. In the end it is better to identify a few key goals and successfully implement them than to attempt to adopt some other company's approach in toto.

STICK WITH TRADITION

Many companies already have succession planning systems. It is likely that the core of most of these systems is a process of identifying potential or probable replacements for specific positions. This is called *replacement planning*.

It's certainly important to have an idea of who may be ready and able to move into a position if it becomes vacant—particularly at senior levels or in functions that have strategic significance. However, building a succession plan around the identification of potential replacements has critical limitations—especially if this is the sole or primary activity a company engages in while preparing for succession.

A replacement planning approach typically has the following steps:

- The top executive assigns the human resource department to ask executives and line managers to identify high-potential people who could replace them in perhaps three to five years.
- HR meets with line managers and executives to discuss their selections and to gather data so that appropriate documentation, such as succession charts, can be completed.
- HR prepares one or more books of information on possible replacements.
- HR subsequently meets annually or at some other regular interval with managers from various levels of the organization to update succession charts and discuss the replacement candidates who have been identified, how they are doing, how close to being ready they are, and so on. Performance appraisal data may be referenced. All this information is kept up to date in a database.
- Material is prepared for a review meeting with top management. Talking points related to potential candidates are identified.

This may seem like a solid approach, and it is in fact a solid *administrative* approach to producing reports for a high-visibility meeting. Whether it serves the goal of ensuring continuity is another question, however.

Here's why: this system is built around preparing for an event rather than focusing on an ongoing process. This means that unless extreme care is taken, the system is more likely to drive preparation of reports than preparation of people for succession. And if the process is to be ongoing, review meetings need to be held more often.

Because this approach focuses on replacement of an incumbent in a current position, it assumes that those naming replacements will be able to predict who can best meet the organization's future business needs. It also assumes that the organization's current structure and strategy will continue indefinitely.

Taking the second point first, this may have been a safe assumption in more stable times, but it certainly isn't now. As for the first point, it is entirely possible to name likely replacements at the lower levels of specific organizational functions, but this approach falters at higher organizational levels, particularly the corporate level. Additionally, this approach can raise questions about the role of diversity—in skills and abilities as well as race and gender—in the company's succession planning process.

The manager of the possible successor simply has a responsibility to report on how or whether someone is developing. If the manager knows what to pay attention to and does so, the discussions between HR and the manager can be helpful and informative for the HR person who is gathering the information. The discussions can be even more useful for the CEO to hear if he or she is taking an active role in the succession planning process.

Finally, in what is essentially an administrative process, HR can become the process owner—and it often does so by default. Administrative processes are often perceived as busywork; facilitating development is not something that most executives or line managers want to do or know how to do. It takes them away from what they and their organizations see as their primary job.

Nevertheless, both research and experience suggest that a succession planning process will not produce the desired results unless the CEO and executive team visibly and actively engage in the process and take responsibility for its outcomes. If a company's top team follows the steps described earlier, the CEO is likely to become aware of only a small subset of the people who should rightfully be considered as having high potential for key executive positions, even if the CEO is actively engaged in the annual review meeting.

TAKE IT FROM HERE

What should a company do about succession planning? Here are some general recommendations:

- Make sure the succession planning process fits the organization. There's nothing wrong with studying successful efforts and identifying specific elements from other organizations that could be adapted and implemented. The danger comes when an entire approach is mandated without weighing what will and will not work in a particular company culture.
- Ensure that roles are clear. HR should act as the facilitator of the succession planning process; the CEO and executive team should own the outcomes. In part this means that the CEO must accept that he or she cannot delegate this role without jeopardizing the success of the process.
- Make development a key element of the process. Focus on developing talent pools instead of just identifying and reporting on possible replacements. Talent pools should contain the diversity necessary to meet unexpected business challenges. If resources are available, broaden the development process.

- Continue to gather and maintain relevant data, but consciously examine and decide what data are relevant and develop systems to provide that data.
- Finally, realize that implementing a succession planning process with development at its core can be a significant change for the entire organization, including HR. It will require time, good planning, regular follow-up, and ongoing support from the top.

Managing Talent Is a Burning Issue in Asia

Michael Jenkins

Bangkok, Jakarta, Mumbai, Shanghai, Singapore—no matter where one works in the Asia-Pacific region, seldom a week goes by without the mail bringing exhortations to attend a presentation, workshop, or seminar on what executives in the region agree is the biggest single challenge facing organizations today in their attempts to execute their vision and strategy: *talent management.* At business breakfasts in major Asian cities, it doesn't take long for businesspeople, after exchanging cards and greetings, to get around to this hot topic. "What are you doing about talent management?" is perhaps the most frequently asked question at such meetings. Leaders are casting about for ideas and inspiration on this issue. With the background of a fast-paced business environment and the known demographics of a shrinking management pipeline, it is not surprising that the issue of talent management keeps leaders in the region awake at night. And unlike some management buzzwords, it seems that *talent management* is here to stay. In fact the issue is likely to become even more urgent, occupying center stage and becoming more worrying in the years ahead.

But what exactly is talent management? For the most part people will likely mention recruitment and retention of able employees as a cornerstone of talent management. Others will point to leadership development as a key piece. But talent management is really an integral part of the vision and strategy of an organization: it's the organization's DNA. Talent management is not merely the recruitment and retention of people that you need here and now; more important, it's an understanding of what the organization is going to need in terms of human resources far into the future. Talent management is the engine of organizational strategy. In Asia today, sophisticated and forward-looking organizations are waking up to the fact that although they might be keeping the lid on current talent needs, that is not going to be enough. A carefully thought-out talent management process will define an organization's ability to deal with challenges—and not just today's challenges, the ones around the corner, but those that may threaten the organization's very existence if something is not done about them *now*.

GREAT DEMAND

So what are the knowns? First, the war for talent is set to intensify. For human resource professionals in China and India it is already a way of life. In China, despite hopes to the contrary, the number of Chinese managers transitioning into positions previously held by foreigners is woefully inadequate. Instead of a diminishment in the number of expensive expatriates in leadership positions, their ranks are on the rise. A leading manufacturer of mobile phones in China recently conceded that demand for expatriate talent—particularly individuals with technical or design expertise—is burgeoning.

In 2004 a study by executive-search firm Heidrick & Struggles estimated turnover among managers in China at 20 percent per year or higher and showed that the average mid- to high-level executive stayed only eight to twelve months in a given position in China. In India, although institutions of higher education produce seemingly vast numbers of information technology personnel, engineers, and business graduates, the word on the street is that the number of people actually deployable is only a fraction of those being brought onto the market.

Also, increasingly advanced skills are required for leading growth and dealing with globalization and rapid technological change. People who can work efficiently across borders and time zones and who can develop fast-reacting, diverse teams in different geographies are in great demand. Not only that, but they *know* they're in great demand, and are more than happy to seek attractive packages from companies eager to take them on. This drives up salaries and intensifies an already dog-eat-dog talent war. It can also depress companies' appetite for costly executive education: why spend resources on someone who might not be around in a year's time?

In addition, the demographics of a retiring baby boom generation and declining birth rates in many (but not all) Asia-Pacific countries increases pressure to obtain the necessary talent from an ever diminishing pool. Talent is becoming more mobile and more inclined to consider working for smaller companies, where the potential for advancement is perceived as greater (although it might not be) and where people feel their voices are more likely to be heard.

Last but not least, increasing awareness of the importance of work-life balance and quality of life makes many executives significantly choosier about where they set down roots. It is not unusual to hear stories of eagerly sought-after business leaders being guided down a delicate recruitment path where the money is right, the work is right, and the ethos of the company is right—but the air quality for their children is not right. Environmental concerns may not seem to be connected with talent management, but think about it: would you want to work in a place that could be detrimental to the health of your family?

MOLDING STRATEGY

So what needs to be done?

At the outset it needs to be recognized that talent management is *not* the same as succession planning. Talent management, done correctly, is a means to create successful organizations for the future. It delves deeper than succession planning because it shapes—and is shaped by—organizational strategy. An organization cannot achieve what it wants to achieve without the right people to not only execute its strategy but also mold and change that strategy to meet the rapidly evolving business and social environment. Research suggests that over the next five years organizations will emphasize pursuing flexible, emergent strategies rather than sticking to stay-the-course strategies. The people who led organizations five years ago will not be the same as those needed to guide work activity five years from now (unless the former people are willing to change).

HIGH POTENTIALS

Drawing a stronger connection between talent management, leadership development, and organizational strategy is arguably the best place to start in attempting to understand how talent management can become the DNA of an organization and how it outweighs succession planning in terms of its long-term significance and impact.

Organizations need to consider the following questions:

- How do we define the quality of leader we need to enact as well as help shape our strategy, knowing that stay-the-course strategies are expected to be supplanted by more flexible, emergent ones?
- How do we identify these leaders? Do we have in-house potential, or do we need to go on a search? Have we established a talent pool?
- Does our current bench strength among our high potentials take sufficient account of what we are going to need in the future as opposed to what we need now?
- Are we moving fast enough to develop this talent? Do we understand what we need to do, and can we do it by ourselves?
- If we recognize that we do not have the capacity to manage talent development internally, how far do we want to go in terms of getting help from outside?

- How able are we to work with external talent developers and take what they offer while marrying that input successfully with what we have created? Can the external talent developers *understand* us?

In many Asia-Pacific organizations the need for talent development is often obscured because management thinks that what is needed is to understand what makes the business's current leaders successful, distill those attributes into a profile, go out and find people who are as close to that profile as possible, hire them, and the talent search is done. This is an approach that emphatically will not work. It will not work because it does not take sufficient account of future needs or the necessity of developing talent at all levels, not just the senior level.

Imaginative organizations are seeing a clear connection between the work of the search firms they contract with and the organizations they bring in to help with leadership development. They are saying, "Let's work with you to identify who will bring value, and if they don't quite have what it takes now, let's work together to develop them." In the years to come, more such creative partnerships and alliances among talent developers can be expected.

Identifying a talent pool of high potentials is nothing new for most organizations, which also realize that investing in these high potentials is a priority. Talent audits designed to uncover overlooked or under-evaluated talent are surfacing in many Asia-Pacific companies. However, there are other issues in the wings. What does the need to build talent and leadership capability at all levels of the organization mean in practice? Where are organizations going to spend their talent-investment dollars, and how will they deal with the majority of individuals who do not make it into the high-potential category? And how can organizations work to enhance the requisite leadership skills of the incumbent senior leadership?

One logical and practical step forward is to define the strategic needs of the organization now and in the future and to measure the degree to which the senior management team is aligned with those needs. A good way to find out where the organization stands is to conduct a *gap study* that ascertains the competencies required to succeed in a specific business or organizational activity and that also measures—using tools such as 360-degree assessments—the extent to which senior leadership meets or falls short of these core criteria for success. Once the senior management team is brought on board, the organization can start to appoint corporate champions who can work with their team leaders to diffuse the core strategic concepts and facilitate a holistic, organization-wide understanding of what's needed in the area of talent for the future.

SETTING PRIORITIES

Clearly, prioritizing efforts is the name of the game. In the corporate context, everyone knows that the cold reality of making the financial numbers (and this is keenly felt in Asian companies) is the primary determinant of the choices companies make. This determining factor originates in the language of the finance department: *what's the return on investment?* Or put another way, what kind of impact can the company expect to get from its talent management systems as a result of the choices it makes? For organizations motivated not merely by profits but also by the extent to which they meet their missions, the same is true. For nongovernmental organizations, maximizing resources is a critical priority: they cannot carry excess luggage.

In the final analysis, whether the organization is for-profit or not-for-profit, there is a critical need for accurate and meaningful assessment of the impact of talent management and leadership development initiatives.

ABOUT THE CONTRIBUTORS

Robin Athey is a senior consultant at Mobius Executive Leadership, a coaching, training and leadership development company.

Vidula Bal is director of global leadership development at Mars Inc. and a former senior faculty member at CCL.

David Baldwin is president, principal consultant, and owner of the Leadership Insight Group, a consulting organization to individuals, teams and organizations. Previously he was a senior faculty member at CCL.

David Berke is a principal at Lorsch, Berke & Associates, a firm that specializes in succession, talent management, and leadership development. Previously he was a senior faculty member at CCL.

Karen Bryson is a former manager of the Leadership Development Program (LDP)® and the Foundations of Leadership program at CCL's San Diego Campus.

Robert Burnside is chief learning officer at Ketchum Inc., a global public relations firm. Previously he was director of the Leadership Innovations Group at CCL.

Maxine A. Dalton is former group director of CCL's Leading in the Context of Difference practice area.

Alessia D'Amato is a fellow in the Employment Relations and Organizational Behavior Group of the Department of Management at the London School of Economics and Political Science. She is a former research associate at CCL.

Kris Downing is director of strategy, planning, and information at CCL.

Kelly M. Hannum is the manager of research in CCL's Global Research Group.

Anjali Hazarika is a senior manager in charge of talent management at Oil India Limited and an adjunct coach with CCL-Asia.

Robert Hogan is president of Hogan Assessment Systems, which uses personality assessments to help companies select employees, develop leaders, and identify talent.

Michael Jenkins is CEO Of Roffey Park Institute, a leadership organization based in the United Kingdom and Singapore. Previously he was CCL's vice president for the Asia-Pacific region.

Robert B. Kaiser is a partner and the director of research and development at Kaplan DeVries, which provides leadership consulting to executives and executive teams.

Gene Klann is owner of Leading With Character, a professional training and coaching firm. Previously he was a senior faculty member at CCL after a twenty-five year career in the U.S. Army.

Michael E. Kossler is director of faculty, design, and delivery at CCL's campus in Singapore.

Karissa McKenna is a former senior program administrator of open-enrollment programs at CCL's campus in San Diego.

Barbara Neisendorf is president of Neisendorf & Associates, a strategic human-resource consulting firm that specializes in helping organizations deliver high performance through their people.

Laura Quinn is manager of design and delivery at CCL's campus in Colorado Springs.

Scott Saslow is founder and executive director of the Institute of Executive Development, an organization that provides resources, networking, and educational events to its membership of more than three thousand executive development professionals.

Stephanie Trovas is a portfolio manager at CCL's campus in San Diego.

Michael Wakefield is president of Xander Inc., a consultancy specializing in the practical application of psychology to leadership and performance enhancement. He is also a principal with Amazon's Global Leadership Development Group. Previously he was manager of trainer development at CCL, where he also designed and delivered customized, client-specific programs.

Ordering Information

To get more information, to order other CCL Press publications, or to find out about bulk-order discounts, please contact us by phone at 336-545-2810 or visit our online bookstore at www.ccl.org/publications.

Lightning Source UK Ltd.
Milton Keynes UK
UKOW031128200213

206498UK00010B/247/P

9 781604 911435